THE PRACTICE
OF CREATIVITY

A Manual for Dynamic
Group Problem-Solving

BY GEORGE M. PRINCE

E P B M

ECHO POINT BOOKS & MEDIA, LLC

www.EchoPointBooks.com

Distributed in the U.S.A. by Lightning Source, Inc.

Cover Design by Trevor Williams
Cover images provided by www.shutterstock.com
Edited by Echo Point Books & Media, LLC

ISBN 978-09638784-8-9 Paperback

Printed in the United States of America

For Mardi, Jon, Wink, and Vick

Contents

Foreward by Steve Krug, author of *Don't Make Me Think*

Preface to 2nd Edition: A Users Perspective: The Synectics Method by Mopsey Strange Kennedy (originally published in *The Boston Globe)*

Author Preface

Epilogue: Discounting/Revenge by George M. Prince

Synecticsworld: Building on The Practice of Creativity

Further Reading

Foreward
by Steve Krug

I don't know about you, but I only learned a few things in college that I've actually used as an adult.

This book is about one of them.

Forty-four years ago, when I was a sophomore at Boston College, I was fortunate enough to meet George Prince and learn about Synectics.

It was quite by accident. I was in an honors program course called Modern Man that counted for half of your credits in the first two years. It was what used to be called a Great Books course: a seminar where you read and discussed seminal literature, from Plato to James Joyce.

But this was 1968, and "relevance" was the hot trend in higher ed, so the powers that be brought in someone to make the program "funkier." This fellow somehow knew George, and persuaded him to give twenty of us a brief introductory course.

So for two nights we found ourselves sitting on the floor in an office in Harvard Square, trying to come up with a better lid for a thermos bottle (see Chapter 2).

I know it doesn't sound like much. But since then, I don't think a week has gone by when I haven't used something I learned in those two evenings.

So, you may ask, what is this Synectics thing? It's most often described as a variation of brainstorming: Alex Osborn's venerable group process for generating new ideas. In classic brainstorming, you gather people in a room and encourage them to toss out as many suggestions as they can (quantity trumps quality), without criticizing other people's contributions or censoring their own. Everything is written down, and only at the end are the best ideas—or combinations of ideas—chosen.

The truth is, brainstorming is fine, but it's really not all that effective. It was used most often in contexts like ad agencies where all you needed to do was generate a catchy tagline, or a single offbeat idea. But it's not that helpful for more challenging problems.

The comparison is apt in one way, though: Synectics does generate new ideas, and plenty of them. Years ago, I used it to run a dozen very successful—and enjoyable—meetings for friends that produced a startling number of rich, novel, and practical solutions to problems ranging from how to finance an independent theater company to how to improve ventilation in a darkroom. And I've used pieces of the Synectics method thousands of times by myself when faced with particularly vexing problems, or backed into a creative corner.

But a more accurate comparison would be brainstorming on steroids—or brainstorming that actually works. And it's also a body of knowledge about how people behave in groups (hint: not very well), and how to create a climate that makes people who are problem-solving together more supportive, productive, and successful. And an awful lot of other things.

It was invented (or discovered, perhaps) back in the 1960's by George and his co-worker William Gordon when they were part of an invention design team at a consulting company called Abt Associates. Clients would bring in their new technology or manufacturing process and the team would come up with products they could be used in. They had a good track record, but it was always hit or miss.

Then one day they had a particularly brilliant idea: they'd record their sessions (on a reel-to-reel tape recorder) and then go back and listen to what they were doing right before they had great ideas.

Based on what they observed, they'd come up with new ways to run their meetings that they thought would increase the behaviors that led to good ideas. Then they'd try using these methods and listen to the new tapes to see which changes worked. Over time, it developed into a full-blown methodology, and they formed their own company—Synectics, Inc.—that ran problem solving sessions for Fortune 500 companies and trained them how to do it themselves. (Full disclosure: I tried to get a job working for them back in the 1980's, but they were only hiring MBAs who could bring in new business.)

One of my favorite examples of the many things they discovered is what eventually came to be called Discount/Revenge. It goes like this: whenever someone (A) puts out an idea, it's extremely likely that someone else in the group (B) will immediately jump in to point out its flaws. This is not done maliciously. In fact, we usually think we're doing it to help the person who made the suggestion. But regardless of the intent, the result is always that A feels like he (or she) has been discounted (or, "dissed" as we might say now). He may not be consciously aware of it, and in fact usually isn't. But if you watch the tape, the next time B makes a suggestion, A will be the first one to find fault with it. Again, not a conscious choice. But stunningly predictable, once you know to look for it.

Try this exercise to see it for yourself: Read Chapter 2, which gives a perfect example of the phenomenon. Then the next time you're sitting in a meeting, keep an eye out for it. Once you're aware of it, you'll see it happening all around you, all day, every day. It's quite impressive to behold, but it's even more impressive to realize that you never noticed it before.

One of the remedies they invented for the Discount Revenge cycle is something I find myself using all the time: the Spectrum Policy (later renamed Itemized Response). It's really very simple:

- You start by assuming that there's a good intent in every suggestion—no matter how boneheaded it may seem to you at first.

- Before you state your reasons why the suggested idea won't work, you have to say two things that you like about it. (This may sound difficult, but it turns out that once you try, it's not that hard.)

- Then—and only then—you can point out the parts that strike you as flawed or impossible. But you have to state these negative concerns not as idea-killers, but as positive goals: new problems to be solved.

Like so many things they came up with, it works amazingly well, and dramatically changes the tone (or what they call the climate) of any meeting.

I can't tell you how happy I am that this book is back in print.

Twelve years ago, when I wrote a book about making Web sites easier to use (*Don't Make Me Think*), I included

The Practice of Creativity in my recommended reading list. It didn't really have anything to do with usability; I was just tossing out a message in a bottle and hoping a few people might get turned on to it as a result. (It was out of print, but it was usually possible to find a used copy on Amazon.)

So I was thrilled when Marshall Glickman wrote me—twelve years later—to tell me he'd found the bottle, read the book, and gotten the rights to reprint it from George's wife, Kathleen Logan-Prince, who was as eager as I was to have people rediscover his work. And I was even more thrilled when he asked me if I'd write an introduction. So here we are.

A word about George: When I was growing up, I used to enjoy the monthly "My Most Unforgettable Character" articles in Reader's Digest, and George would have made an excellent subject. I was fortunate enough to spend some time with him when he let me talk my way into some advanced training classes years after we first met. He was an imposing presence (what you might refer to as "a big lug"), but he had a wonderful gentle quality about him. More than anyone else I've met, you knew the creative wheels were always turning, and he wanted you to be a better you.

I hope this book will give you a glimpse into his remarkable mind, and some slight sense of his equally remarkable spirit. Enjoy.

Steve Krug
Brookline, Massachusetts
June 2012

Steve Krug is the Author of *Don't Make Me Think: A Common Sense Approach to Web Usability* and *Rocket Surgery Made Easy: The Do-It-Yourself Guide to Finding and Fixing Usability Problems*. He is a usability consultant who has more than 20 years of experience as a user advocate for companies like Apple, Netscape, AOL, Lexus, and others. Based in part on the success of his first book he has become a highly sought-after speaker on usability design. And based on our experience working with him at Echo Point, he's also a super nice and likeable guy.

THE SYNECTICS METHOD

"I see a Bumblebee falling in love" and other insights on the practical path to solving real-world problems.

By Mopsy Strange Kennedy

Originally published in the Boston Globe

Seven men are sitting in a room together, one of them gnarling his thoughts in a display of game-show intensity while the others pop out words, slowly, sharply, like the balls in a pinball machine. "I see a bumblebee falling in love with an elephant." Feverishly, and with great appreciation, a man who is standing up writes it down on one of the many pulp pads nailed to the wall.

"Good," he says. "Any more?"

Someone else speaks up. "Well, it's a build. Can I do that?"

"Sure," says the standing man holding the crayon.

"I'm thinking that a bumble-bee stings you and it hurts, but ultimately the pain can bring pleasure."

"Uh-huh," says the standing man, writing it all down on the pad. "Is there more to that one?" "Well, sometimes a little thing like a bumblebee can only get the attention of something very large, like an elephant, by hurting it a little, and that wakes up the elephant and makes it more sensitive."

Another voice comes in. "Something about honey ... sweet ... a bee is both a stinger and producer of something sweet. Somehow the sting has to come first and then the honey will follow."

IMAGINATION-SQUEEZING

These people squeezing their imaginations, aching for connections between words and ideas and images like charade players are in reality not seven Kurt Vonneguts or a bunch of advertising copywriters. They are sobersided businessmen who have come for a week of training in "creative problem-solving," at Synectics, Inc., a firm in Cambridge that teaches a method called Synectics. And all this shaggy-dog thinking is part of an elaborate mental detour that ultimately relates back to ordinary business problems, such as:

How can my small company join forces effectively with a much larger one? Hence bumblebee; hence elephants. Later in the process, when they come down from the high of free association, the bumblebee and the elephant will be demetaphorized and reunited with their referents, company A and company B, and turned into a practical critique that the man who brought the problem can take back and use.

Synectics, not surprisingly, is the invention of inventors, two men who worked at Arthur D. Little. In the course of working on a safe cigarette, a non-fatiguing metal skin for airplanes, and a method of packing fragile things in pliable, fast-drying foam they became concerned with the question of creative states of mind and how to get them. They were also interested in the particular knot of events that define a situation when anyone working on a problem gets stuck. "When someone says they're stuck," one of them said, "them's fighting words to us."

George Prince, a creative man in advertising-turned-inventor, is one of the founders and now chairman of the company. Because he and his staff find paradoxes useful (and use them), I will call him pliably concrete. It's unusual to find a man in his position whose way of thinking is so prone to speculation, garden-path diversions and self-questioning, but, on the other hand, he's made them his business. Subjunctive thinking is a way of life for him.

"I had been in psychoanalysis, and one thing I learned was that we don't do things for rational reasons," said George. This tolerance, even preference, for the irrational led him into wondering what irrational forces were so conducive to invention and creativity. He found that thinking in metaphors, going off into the wild blue yonder from the terrestrial matter at hand, is often the source of amazing creative sparks and connections. That, and a real openness to what he calls approximate thinking, became, as it were, the foam that he quick dried into the Synectics system. He has since transmitted it to thousands of business-people and used it in "problem labs" with companies to break impasses and forge inventions. The very word Synectics means "the tying together of seemingly unrelated elements," and it also conveniently describes the method of bringing unrelated people to work together in groups.

But as George Prince said, creativity involves risk, and so he was equally interested in the psychological factors that enhance or destroy meetings and personal relations in general. Perhaps one could say that his actual inventions were just vehicles for the discovery of the mysterious currents passing between people working on a problem. "I had been watching tapes of hundreds of meetings to find out how to be productive and what it was that inhibited their probability of success. This man, Bob Goulding, had been doing Transactional Analysis and looking at the same thing—transactions—from a mental health point of view. When I heard of him I said, "We've got to get him."

In looking at these meeting tapes, Prince saw that "there are ways that people transact that reduce their willingness to work together. In unraveling that process we discovered people are fantastically sensitive—far beyond anything we recognize—and if I put you down even slightly, you'll compute that, and if possible, even below your awareness, you'll get back at me or at somebody. This is generally not recognized by the people who are doing it—cultural static hides it—and people say, 'We're mature, and I can tell you that your idea is rotten.' But no one acknowledges the put-down."

The cure for this disease of cruelty that bolluxes meetings and inventions first came intuitively and magically, as in Biofeedback, where you don't know quite what you're doing right, and basically consisted of giving everyone a full and distinct role, and of building into the structure a place for all present ideas to germinate if they can.

"My then-partner Bill Gordon was very skillful at running a meeting successfully, and we watched tapes of our meetings with our big client, Johns-Manville. First we said, 'Watch us and do it that way,' and then we began building around that." These two men, as Prince tells it, "weren't behaving ourselves at Arthur D. Little. We worked odd hours. They wanted us to stop this unorthodox stuff because it caused trouble with other people there who wanted to work like us. So we left, and took some of our clients with us."

Synectics calls itself a mildly dogmatic system, and that dogma incorporates, especially in the Itemized Response, which emphasizes the constructive element, Prince's passionate belief in positivism. But it is also a matter of taste and style—on one level not so vulgar as to need saying, but on another level often expressed during the week of training. It comes out in the high level of sophistication in the trainers (which goes a long way toward dispelling fears of crackpotism), in the atmosphere in the Church street office in Cambridge, which is chic and not very like an office, and in an assumption that we are all gentlemen here (unless we are ladies)."

George's Archimedes-in-the-bathtub breakthrough came when he discovered, by tracking the thought processes in an especially fruitful meeting, that the images, metaphors and verbal or visual connections between seemingly unrelated things were often at the base of an innovative idea. Metaphor-thinking, it was explained, has accounted for many inventions, and more so since there has been this disciplined system for evoking it.

A glassmaker named Pilkington had an epiphany at the kitchen sink when he watched droplets of grease rise to the top of the water. By forcing this image onto the question of making glass, he came up with an idea for something called float glass, which revolutionized the industry (and, we are told, "made a lot of money for him too").

The week-long course—the Open Course—that I took was populated almost entirely by people who worked for large companies (one described himself as Mr. Plastics, another as Mr. Steel). Their companies had given them time off and paid the bill, a biting $800 – no mean mark for faith. Many of them were not the first person in their firm to take the course, and the theory in sending them was to have yet another person in the company spread Synectics among their coworkers. All of them, including myself, were told to bring in two problems— real ones— to practice on. Since I don't tend to have marketing problems, I tried to get away from the more squishy personal problems I traffic in. The Synectics approach hardly smacked of psychotherapy, and I imagined that only the most objective problems would do, but I was wrong. The problems the participants brought were incredibly diverse: How to invent a better diaper, How to make an infinite number of colors of telephones available, How to build a strong organization in Spain and reorganize one's personal life in a short time, How to get out of the office boy syndrome and gain management recognition, How not to be left out of a group of people renting a house together at the beach.

But to discover what we had to learn we were first introduced to what we had already in terms of our skills, tendencies, approaches, and the like, in meetings and in the generating of ideas. In groups of seven we were put into rooms, where we were videotaped discussing the question: How to invent a safe circular saw? This meeting was like an initial weigh-in in a diet class, showing us where we were and what it was we had to lose. Almost any meeting—and ours was no exception—has limits and difficulties that the Synectics method is designed to overcome. These include a headlong scurrying for power; a tendency to reject ideas that are too far out (and often to reject the proposer of the idea as well), an endless redefining of the problem, a subtle lack of support of each other's ideas, a need to go prematurely for the most obviously sensible idea, and a general confusion of roles. There is also, I am told, a tendency to reject ideas put forth by women when the subject is in any way scientific or technological. I would add that I took my own lambs to the slaughter by saying, "I don't know a thing about machinery" before each idea I advanced, though by the end of the course I had come to see the irrelevance of that disclaimer.

As we looked at the tape of our meeting, seemingly quite civilized even if we didn't come up with a real solution, it was amazing to see how seven random, on-their-guard people managed to fall into these common traps almost automatically. Our leader, Jit Chopra—an executive vice-president—went through the tape, pointing out where questions were asked that were really veiled timorous ideas trying themselves out in the form of pseudo-queries. Jokes that actually contained embryonic ideas were discounted out of existence, and anything that didn't seem to bear on the problem was summarily dismissed. And, maybe most typically, ideas that were only partial were ruled out simply because they were incomplete.

One might imagine that an ever more streamlined efficiency would be the prescribed cure for all of this; in fact, it's just the opposite. Synectics at its most typical is a permission to expand into the lunatic spheres of thinking and imagining, an invitation to billow.

"So often," Jit explained to us, "people are in a win-lose situation in meetings like this. It's possible to structure it so that it comes out win-win by building constructively on any idea, seeing the good in it and isolating what needs further work." He was leading into one of Synectics most important concepts:

the Itemized Response. According to this system, if you suggest an idea to me I will give you three things I like about it. This leaves the chewy gristle, the problematical part, which, instead of rejecting, I state as a "concern" or, better yet, as a "wish" I have about the idea that will either trim its disadvantages or expand its good potential.

By using this approach, Synectics has banished the dragging, dead-end features of a respondents negative view of an idea. By going at a problem in this way, one can carve a hole in one's misgivings about a given idea that will lead into a more spacious positive zone of thinking. The "trouble" with an idea becomes its new point of growth.

Next we were introduced into the basic structure of a Synectics meeting, wherein the leader is split into two people: the Content Leader, or the client who might come in with a problem; and the Process Leader, or leader, who organizes the meeting around the client. The other five people are the participants—maybe the juiciest role. In contrast to common practice, the five people who help the client with his problem are not necessarily experts; for example, at NASA, highly technical people worked with housewives who knew nothing whatsoever about space technology.

By isolating these roles and giving everybody a distinct

function, you eliminate "leading from the floor," kowtowing to the boss, and losing sight of the true client. In a really tight Synectics session, you are straining at the straps as it is to fulfill your own role, so usurping another person's is almost out of the question by the very nature of the design.

The ubiquitous props at Synectics are reams and reams of pulp pads that hang on the wall. Ideas are written on them; then the top sheet is removed and stuck on the wall, making a crayoned tapestry. After our first preconversion blunder into the circular saw problem and a discussion of the Synectics method of doing things, we chose another problem from our group and marched into Room A, where we had half an hour to come up with a solution.

The client, or owner of the problem, had huddled with the leader for a few minutes first; then the time was wound up and the rest of us anxious harpies were introduced to the Problem as Given, as it's called, though not a business one in this case: How to keep my dog from dragging home slimy dead things. After a brief analysis of the problem, a look at what he'd already tried in the past, and what he hoped to get out of this session, the five of us began scribbling our Goals and Wishes on our legal pads.

The Goal/Wish is the name Synectics people give the speculative, avowedly half-baked, semiloony arrows pointing vaguely in the direction of a solution to the problem. The very things that are so often strong-armed out of a problem-solving session are here positively invited and nurtured into existence. "Make it strange—be wishful," the leader repeatedly said. If anything was slightly discouraged, it was the over-literal, wrapped and delivered "answer."

Goal/Wishes spurted from our minds onto our legal pads and from there up to the pulp pads on the wall. The fact that the problem at hand was of a personal rather than a straight business nature mattered not at all; the process was the same. Goal/Wishes, like the Problem as Given itself, always begin with "How to...": How to make the dog hate the slimy dead things, How to Make your housemates like the smell, How to perfume your dog, How to enclose an area for him, How to buy a cat instead, How to make the smell itch (the contributor who gave this Goal/Wish was beginning to edge into the particular surrealism that the method encourages), How to make your dog want to get clean, How to enclose your dog without buying hundreds of yards of fencing, and so on. The ideas flew out uncensored, though at first we were a bit too timorous, not yet masters of the wonderfully off-the-wall suggestions that grow like weeds in the soil of Synectics. The leader, ideally, kneels, pleads, eyeballs, stimulates, encourages, and tugs both the client and the participants into greedy, energetic thinking.

The dog-owning client looked around at the suggestions that had been written on the wall on pulp pads, and picked and threaded them together until he came up with "an Idea," which is closer to the germ of a possible Possible Solution. He then paraphrased the idea, using what are called creative misunderstandings, adding to it with the help of the participants, molding the idea anxiously until it had some shape. "Give me the Itemized Response on the idea you've got there," said our leader, and the client came up with the three things he liked about the idea. If only two had been forthcoming, a third would have virtually been dragged out of him. Then he started his concern or difficulty with the idea, always bearing the winged feet of a Wish.

"Can you think of how you might overcome that concern or implement that wish?" the leader asked, and something in the tension of the atmosphere, the positive cast of thought flipping all negatives into positives, helped the client come up with a suggestion that would blitz the concern. "Does this look like a Possible Solution?" he was asked.

"Yes," said the client.

"Is it new? Is it feasible? Do you know the next steps you will have to take to work on it?"

The client lightly elaborated these steps. And if everything went according to the plan—seventeen minutes by the anxiously ticking clock—the buzzer went off, the idea sheets were ripped from the walls and handed to the client, and we went to watch the videotape of what had just transpired.

These things—the Excursion, Imaging, and the Absurd Connection—were introduced the third day of the course, by which time the initial inhibitions were lowered and the shirttails of wishing were already flapping in the breeze. Dealing with someone else's problem, How to make an infinite number of telephone colors available to our customers, we went through the process of writing down Goal/Wishes (How to have the colors snap on, How to paint the phone yourself, etc.). Then we took one word out of one Goal/Wish and went along blindly associating, utterly forgetting the problem as we went. How to make light-sensitive phones like sunglasses was one suggestion.

The word "light" was randomly picked, like a card in a card trick, and we went along with light ... bulb ... tulip ... mouth ... teeth ... white ... black ... magic ... rabbit ... hutch. Of these the word "magic" was chosen – and proved to be almost too loaded; the results were more amazing when the word we started from was quite banal. We were instructed to think in the most "absurd" way possible about how magic could be brought to bear on the problem of these phones.

We began to "image" off of "magic"; that is, produce associations to that word.

"I see many-colored scarves; one side is yellow and one side is blue" some said.

"A magician is a charlatan; he fakes his tricks, they're not real."

"A magician saws women in half. Maybe he could pull scarves out of her when she is in two."

"How about the idea that the scarves, the rabbits, and the women in two pieces are all real but the magician is fake, just a dummy."

"Magicians have the power to make elements disappear and appear."

"I'm thinking of the Wizard of Oz, who was sort of a charlatan who everyone believed in."

The man with the problem was asked to look at the images written on the idea sheets and try to make what is called an Absurd Connection between one of those vignettes and the problem of the telephone. "Try to come up with something so crazy that if you suggested it to your boss you could get fired immediately. We call this the Get-Fired Solution."

The client, a man from Canada, strained in his seat. "Something about color freedom. I see that the phone could be fun because you don't quite know what it's going to do. There is a surprise element that takes it from the utilitarian to the amusing. It has a presto-changeo quality."

We began to work on the idea, thinking about magic and telephone color. Someone suggested a kaleidoscope; someone else suggested a jukebox with its swirling rainbows, and someone recalled those pillows of margarine from World War II that contained a pellet of color you would squeeze all through it. That appeared to be force-able onto one possible solution. Another idea was to have the phones made of something that changes color when stress is externally applied (a little diversionary toy that works this way was described).

He Itemized his Response to the idea and isolated the areas he would have to work on, and our first Imaging session was over.

People are reluctant to think in a way that flies in the face of things they are knowledge-able about at first," said Prince. "They're unwilling to take chances even when there's no risk, but we give them permission to think speculatively in a way-out way." In my week at Synectics, I was amazed at how quickly the people burst out of their accustomed framework of thinking and their work vo-cabulary (heavy with feedback, input, cost analysis, in-depth marketing surveys, and interfac-ing) and into this other, comfort-ably structured but nevertheless wacky cast of thought. There was only one man who violently fought the Synectics idea that the technically sophisticated could work beside the untutored and get something from them, but the week taught him otherwise. "Doing" Synectics restores one's faith that it is out of the mouths of babes, nonscientists, and outsiders of any stripe that good ideas can come. In fact it gave me a whole new dangerous feeling that I could be an inventor. I found—the way I often look at a punch line of a joke and wonder how the writer went through the middle steps to get there—that Synectics has caused me to look at soap bottle tops, car washes, bureaucratic practices, and trick ashtrays with the same curiosity, wondering what dazzling Synectics leap might have spurred the invention. (One can imagine: "But, Daddy, why can't I see the picture now?" "Until I invent the Polaroid camera, you'll have to make do with what there is.")

The Imaging, Absurd Connection, and force-fit of the possible solution onto the problem are the tamest methods in that line. There is also the Essential Paradox, where you work with a word in the list of Goal/Wishes and turn it into a paradox. Thus, if the word was branch, as in *branch* of a tree, the essential paradox might be "independently integral" and you would work that into your solution somehow. Personal Analogy, where you "become" the object you're working on (as in Gestalt therapy); Picture-making, where you draw a doodle and search for an image in it; Cloud Watching, where you find an image in the clouds; and Take a Walk, where you take a key word and then walk down the street looking for instances of your key word, which, again, you apply to the problem.

We were shown a film using more arcane methods, where the client—a consultant who wanted to attract business without looking desperate— went through a roller-coaster ride of images from inanimate nature. She finally settled on "thunderclap," which she took through a personal analogy ("I feel exhilarated stage-fright with this electricity") and then through a series of wildly wandering thoughts that came to the idea of "lightning never strikes twice" and from there the idea that she could present her business as something that was offered once, and never again. The idea she evolved was that she could change—through a shift in the marketing technique—from appearing to be the supplicant to coming across as the bountiful offerer of a hot but evaporating opportunity.

Although hundreds of people have come to Synectics, and they in turn have spread the word to more thousands of their coworkers, it would be wrong to say that Synectics hasn't had to fight for its credibility. Luckily, many of the people who work for the company come from the hard-headed world of science, which helps (a few dropouts from electronics, another from architecture). "At first it was hard to sell the course, and I reacted very defensively," said

Prince. "There's the Open Course, but there's also the Problem Lab where people come from a company with a specific problem they want help on." But even then they sometimes resist the method, pretending it's just like the way they work back home—which is improbable. "When people give all kinds of signals that they're going to fight it, we have to work extra hard to show them just how and why our method is so effective." One way is to run a "before," as we did with the circular saw problem. (Synectics, by the way, works in client organizations that are highly confidential, but a few, such as this one, have been cleared for hypothetical "play" in sessions.) Seeing exactly how they blunder along is often enough to show a company that there might be at least one other way. (Nothing is brand new under the sun, of course; there's a method called Kepnor-Tregoe, and another called Brainstorming, which also address themselves to problem-solving.)

Of the companies that have consulted Synectics, the most famous are Kimberly-Clark, which invented its space-saved box through this method; Ford, which discovered a new way to suspend four wheels evenly; Union Carbide, which found a new method for removing residue after boiling steel; and NASA, which got, with the help of those housewives, some highly technical innovative ideas.

The Nestle Company found the process useful (though what they came up with is still under wraps), and in doing market research the Synectics format has rendered the business of interviewing laypeople far swifter and more focused.

"Anyone confronted with a new test product can tell you what they like about it," said Hank Jendras, "but the negative is harder. We've turned it around through the Itemized Response so that when they say, 'I hate the bitter taste of this chocolate,' it can come out, instead, as a Wish: 'I wish it tasted better or sweeter.' If we waited for them to spontaneously tell us all sides of their response it would be far less efficient, and this way we can go right to the heart of the matter."

Different features of the system get taken home and integrated—not always with great orthodoxy—by the various companies that come to Synectics. Westinghouse Credit Corporation, with no product of a palpable nature, has emphasized, as James Meston said, "exploding new ideas to the point where we have been able to come up with new ways to finance new levels of business. For them," he said, "the most useful thing has been the aspect of the system that reduces or eliminates the domineering 'man with power,' who subtly shuts off other people's ideas."

He also pointed out that although initially it's hard for people in the real world to think this way, "Synectics makes it possible for even very practical businesspeople to be loose and playful and wishful and to tap into the creative right hemisphere of the brain. Nowadays everything you read talks about the right hemisphere, but Synectics really had a quarter on that when they started out, and it's affected our way of working"

Synectics has a sly but practical way of dealing with the problem of keeping the faith and using the method on people back at the ranch who are uninitiated in the system and who may be hostile to it. Hence Guerilla Synectics, a way of surreptitiously "doing" a Synectics session on people when there is no permission to do and no knowledge of the hidden Johnny Appleseed in their midst. It consists of subtly shuttling back and forth between the various roles, becoming first the leader, then the client, milking ideas and organizing them. "I listen like a bandit for Goal/Wishes," says Jit Chopra in a discussion of Guerrilla Synectics, "because people generate them all the time without calling them that. And I can do an Itemized Response to my own ideas and other people's even when they don't know what that is. You can also use this method on children. You can draw Goal/Wishes out of them and you can itemize your response to their wishes in a way that doesn't threaten them."

George Prince acknowledged his indebtedness to children because of their masterful use, as he put it, of "approximate versus precise thinking." A baby who sucks his thumb as he holds a fistful of scrambled egg is "permitting" himself to capitalize on the on the piece of the motion that is workable, and because he doesn't censure himself for the sloppy outcome, he is able to experiment further and learn—as we all know—with a rapidity that puts adult learners to shame.

Synectics wouldn't be Synectics if everything up their sleeve had been pulled out. George is working on something called Mindspring Theory, which further develops the idea that the mind is an eternal spring full of nourishing ideas. There is a workbook by Bill Gordon (who is no longer at Synectics) called Making It Strange.

How to Itemize my Response to Synectics (we were given, upon departure, buttons that say I Think, Therefore IR)? I would first say it was fun. ("May I say something non-goal oriented?" "Please do.") Second, I'd say I liked it because it bore a pleasant similarity to dreaming, in that what looked like loose information was made into something patterned and useful. And third, it got me thinking about thinking. ("Can you say more?") Well, it showed me that many hitherto remote questions related to business and science could be made understandable or even lovable. "Such as?" Well, I wish there were some way I could apply this thinking to some money-making scheme. How about an electronic fist that jumps out of the front door and socks burglars and encyclopedia salesman? How about a way of playing life's film backwards— as in Mary Poppins—so an avalanche of clothes could fold themselves in mid-air and pop back into the cupboard nearly of their own accord? But even barring all that, "knowing" Synectics, one can have the ongoing pleasure of mentally unraveling existing inventions and wishfully reconstructing them back into existence in a new form. Now there's the wheel ... but if I take a walk I might come up with an improved wheel....

Mopsy Strange Kennedy is a free-lance writer who lives in Cambridge.

Preface

In 1951, as a result of becoming newly familiar with the work of Jung and Freud and thus with the principles of psychoanalysis, I became convinced that imagination and the creation of ideas could be stimulated by the proper use of repressed thoughts. An executive in an advertising and marketing company, I began experimenting with psychologists and creative people on everyday problems to find out if and how new ideas could be so generated.

In 1958 I met W. J. J. Gordon of the Invention Design Group of Arthur D. Little, an industrial-research company. Mr. Gordon not only agreed that ideas could be deliberately stimulated but also believed he knew the elements necessary to do so. Further, he had a system for producing these stimuli, which he called Operational Creativity. His system made use of certain psychological states that he believed were vital to creativity: detachment, deferment, and speculation, among others. This was a quantum jump beyond my own thinking. In addition, Gordon had conceived of using a tape recorder to examine how groups work, by discovering through replays what actually was said, done, and achieved—much as football coaches use slow-motion game films.

I joined Mr. Gordon at Arthur D. Little as part of a group of eight men whose job it was to develop new or improved products, processes, and procedures for client companies. As workers in the invention business, we conceived of products and then made prototypes or models in our laboratory. Adopting what *now* seems a simple and obvious idea, we used a tape recorder (and in time, video tapes) at our many meeting. It became our obsession to discover why we were sometimes successful and sometimes not—to determine what procedures lead to creativity.

In 1960 we left Arthur D. Little to start our own company, Synectics Inc., devoted to invention, research into the inventive process, and teaching. The first published report of our findings appeared in 1961, in *Synectics*, written by Mr. Gordon.

A venture that provides the sort of information contained in *The Practice of Creativity* requires the support of many men who see promise in small amounts of data and are willing to join the experiment as learners. Of course, these clients became our greatest teachers, and many of them continue to be. Without them this book would not exist.

The foundation for many of the elements described in *The Practice of Creativity* came about in the years 1958 to 1965, when I worked closely with Mr. Gordon. His many contributions are much appreciated.

Cavas M. Gobhai has been an active participant in our research, teaching, and Problem Laboratories since 1963. Almost every new understanding of the creative process that I discuss here contains a measure of his thinking. Often he was the first to see an emerging pattern that we could elaborate and experiment with.

I am particularly fortunate to have had Peter A. Bergson working with me. It is largely due to his efforts that this book exists in its present form. He not only combined our former course text with present teaching practices but also contributed many original suggestions throughout.

Amarjit Chopra, a colleague, has made many valuable contributions. His thinking about the competitive nature of meetings and the win-or-lose aspects have been particularly helpful.

Dean L. Gitter worked with Mr. Gordon and me from

1963 to 1966. His energy and insightful observations greatly added to what we have learned.

Josephine O'B. Power has also been a valued contributor both in teaching and in construction of the book. Carol Bruno's attention to rewriting, ordering, and typing has been invaluable.

I would like to acknowledge the many helpful suggestions of Martin T. Orne, C. R. Sperry, and Jonathan M. Prince. Norbert Slepyan made contributions far beyond the call of duty as editor, and I am grateful. Finally I want to thank Mardi Prince, my wife, who watched and applauded with pleased amazement as this book went from draft to draft.

G.M.P.

Cambridge, Massachusetts
1970

CREATIVITY: an arbitrary harmony, an expected astonishment, a habitual revelation, a familiar surprise, a generous selfishness, an unexpected certainty, a formable stubbornness, a vital triviality, a disciplined freedom, an intoxicating steadiness, a repeated initiation, a difficult delight, a predictable gamble, an ephemeral solidity, a unifying difference, a demanding satisfier, a miraculous expectation, an accustomed amazement.

1
Needed: Dependable Creativity

Change has become the dominant concern of top management, and growth plans are geared to projected changes in wealth, technology, demand patterns, birth rate, habit, taste, population distribution, power supply, raw material production, and other such considerations. As these factors change, so the firm's activities must change to meet them; and change can be of only two kinds—imitative or creative. You can change the way other people have changed already, or you can change in a new way. You can follow, or you can lead. You can wait until you find out how other firms have coped with or exploited the projected changes, and then copy them, or you can think up original ideas that they have not hit on. And if you do that, you are being creative in the fullest sense. Change is not a sideline in the business of leadership, it is integral to the whole idea: to describe a man who left things exactly as he found them as a "great leader" would be a contradiction in terms. A leader may change the map of Europe, or the breakfast habits of a nation, or the capital structure of an engineering corporation; but changing things is central to leadership, and changing them before anyone else is creativeness.[1]

In his inner heart, each of us knows that he is capable of great deeds. To watch any six-year-old build a dream world and courageously overcome some powerful threat to it against great odds is to see such confidence in operation. This capacity stays with us in the adult world but is discouraged as it is buried by repeated bad examples set by our elders and betters. When *we* are gradually transformed into the elders and betters, all but a few of us

[1] Antony Jay, *Management and Machiavelli*, pp. 82–83.

forget or write off our ability for great achievement. We make a virtue of adult consistency and rigidity; we diminish our ability to grow and to change; we find that while our eye was upon imitating adulthood, we have let slip our grasp of originality. We need to rediscover how to change so as to renew our ability to solve problems in original, satisfying ways rather than persisting in imitation and passive acceptance.

Most of our institutions are patterned after the family structure. The father or mother is boss and the other members do as he or she says. In business the boss or manager takes charge. *Presumably* he is responsive to his people's needs.

In recent years we have watched a breakdown of this pattern, civil disobedience and student riots being familiar examples. This breakdown is consistent with what we see in industry, though the revolt against the traditional manager is not yet clear—except when examined on tape, where careful inquiry reveals a deep dissatisfaction with leaders. Subordinates tend to feel manipulated, helpless, and underused. Yet, in employment advertisements we see a lot about challenging assignments and opportunities to run one's own show.

I believe that the real challenge is to develop a different sort of show, one in which a manager knows his true function with some precision. This function is *not* to get things done *through* people. It is to make genuine use of people: first to discover what should be done and next to discover how to get it done with the most satisfaction for all involved.

We are beginning to find out how to develop this new kind of leader. The skills required are considerable.

The role of manager in today's business, church, and political system has evolved from the past. We hear of the professional manager, and we see an enormous growth in undergraduate and graduate training to produce these professionals. These highly skilled people have made United States industry an astonishing force for productivity. There is no question about the material effectiveness of the system: the quality of the life it produces for those involved, however, needs looking into.

If, as I believe, each man and woman is a born creative problem solver, such potential demands expression and exercise. Creativity in products, production, and marketing have put us in the position we are in today. The evidence that the "mass of men lead lives of quiet desperation" begs us to use more of our creative potential in attacking problems of work dissatisfaction and prejudice and even applying new solutions to underdeveloped countries and foreign relations. Here we have the makings of a satisfying revolution: on the one hand we have problems (opportunities) of defiant size and complexity; on the other we have creative talents that cry to be used. Synectics is an attempt to bring these two resources together.

When we began our research, we originally thought of the group as a means of making the creative process visible so we could examine it; the meeting itself, the way people worked together, grew in importance in our concerns until it more than equaled the procedures for developing ideas. Because of what we heard and saw happening, we have had to question many basic assumptions about meetings and, in particular, meeting leadership. Many observations surprised us; their sum strongly suggests that the traditional problem-solving meeting is a blunt instrument, not an incisive one.

One of the first handicaps is that meetings are often used casually so that either there is only a vague notion about the objective or the objectives are mixed. The chairman may want to give information, get ideas, and see how members react to some ideas of his own. None of these objectives may be wrong, but without precise knowledge of what is expected of them, members easily get confused. An agenda alone does not solve this problem.

Second, meetings are frequently used to solve problems, to plan, and to help make decisions. Creativity is a vital component because it develops alternatives, enriches possibilities, and imagines consequences. There is evidence, however, that chairmen unwittingly discourage creativity and free speculation.

Third, leaders use their power unwisely. The leader is often the senior member or boss and has influence that transcends his importance in the meeting. It is accepted practice for him to use this power and for other members to play to it. Thus the leader's prejudices can get in the way of open proposals of alternatives.

Fourth, a common hindrance is antagonism toward ideas. Mr. A says, "I think it would be a good idea to shape our dog food like a bone and make it chewier." Mr. B says, "There is already a dog bone on the market." Mr. C says, "And also one of the strengths of the competition, Gainesburgers, is that they are like hamburgers—not chewy." Problems and opportunities tend to be dealt with by this kind of exchange. Both the idea of a new shape and a new texture are worth exploration, but the possible good in what Mr. A says is attacked and the chance to develop an alternative is wasted.

There are other built-in drawbacks in the traditional meeting, but all can be reduced or eliminated by the chairman or leader. To do so he must develop a model to help him recognize helpful and destructive actions and know how to use or discourage them.

The logic of a meeting is simple and sound. A person needs the help of other minds. He invites them to a meeting. They come. Very quickly the behavior of the meeting members fails to support the logical meeting model. As suggested above, antagonism, defensiveness, individual effort, and confusion about purpose interfere with accomplishment.

HYPOTHESIS FOR A MEETING MODEL

If one peers objectively through the cultural camouflage at recurring patterns of behavior in meetings, there emerges in each person a paradoxical combination of two major elements, sensitivity and aggressiveness, which seems unfortunate and whimsically destructive. But these are precisely the qualities needed for inspired problem solving. Aggressiveness presses us to adventure beyond the rules, to speculate outrageously. Sensitivity alerts us to both opportunities and shortcomings. Like most powerful weapons, these can be used destructively. It is up to the meeting leader to prevent careless misuse, and eventually, as an individual becomes informed about the far-reaching consequences of the improper application of his talents, he will police himself.

We find it useful to assume that every participant unconsciously perceives a meeting as a competition between himself and everyone else. The rules of competition apply: if someone else wins, he will lose. To make life even more hazardous he brings with him into the meeting a delicate image of himself. Any disparagement or put-down will damage this image. When this happens (given the competition, it is very likely), his total attention and skills are devoted to repairing and refurbishing his image, preferably at the expense of his rival.

USING THE NEW MODEL

A good leader with this model in mind sets top priority on the defense of each person's image of himself. He knows that each member cherishes his own individuality above any problem to be solved. If this quality is threatened, the member not only stops cooperating, he becomes dangerous to the purposes of the meeting. To prevent this the leader repeatedly demonstrates that in this meeting no images will be damaged, no one is going to lose.

His next priority is to direct the aggression where it belongs: against the problem.

His third priority is to demonstrate that in this meeting not only does no one lose, but everyone wins.

The effective leader's actions tell each member of his team, "I will not permit you to be attacked so you need not be concerned with defensiveness." "Concentrate your attacks on the problem, not on the people." "I am going to honor and help use every contribution you make. You are going to win with contributions."

A successful meeting depends upon intense cooperation and teamwork, but activities must proceed in a way that will enhance individuality, never submerge it.

The group rotates its leadership so that each member experiences the role of leader as well as that of participant. When the group member is acting as leader he uses his individuality to serve the creative surge of the group. While the group members are roving freely in their imaginations, the leader is watching, recording, and keeping to a plan.

Each member develops his own style but recognizes the importance of every other teammate. Learning to be a good meeting participant is as rewarding as learning to be a good leader. Discovering how to use associatory words and thoughts in a freely deliberate manner is as valuable in everyday living as in group problem solving.

Our experiments with creative group leadership make it clear that the leader can multiply the effectiveness of the participants. This requires a fresh examination of the role of leader or chairman. The basic element is power to control. We have found that if the leader uses his position to serve himself—for example, to get support for an idea of his own—each member reacts by serving *himself:* promoting his own idea, looking for flaws in the notions of others, and other divisive activities aimed at the building and defense of his own image. If the leader demonstrates that his power will be used to serve group members, to assure each idea a hearing, to give support and consideration to each thought, the members can concentrate on producing such thinking. In this sense the leader is servant to the individuals in the group, and the group is servant to the task of the meeting. The leader's whole attention is devoted to helping the group use its wits. In addition, it is important that everyone regularly has the opportunity to lead: to test and shape his capability and taste the responsibility of meeting leadership.

The role of the leader is different from the traditional role of the strong chairman, who points directions, makes instant judgments of relevance and usefulness, hews to the agenda, and parcels out assignments. All these activities are important, but each must be re-examined and used only when appropriate. Very few leaders of traditional meetings are able consistently to sort out helpful responses from damaging ones. Further, it seems that most of the time the leader (and the manager) does not specifically know what his role should be. He has a general goal: to get things done. He assumes that the present structure of chairman, agenda, and guided (or perhaps free-wheeling) discussion is effective. These assumptions go unexamined because things *do* get done, goals *are* accomplished. But our observations suggest that an uninformed meeting leader wastes his own and his group's talent by allowing destructive behavior to subvert and blur the meeting's focus. Such waste is expensive. Boredom and impatience are familiar symptoms; less obvious to the unawakened eye are hostility and rivalry.

The traditional leader tends to be self-serving and manipulative. For example, his own ideas get special treatment because he gravitates toward responses that support his own preconceived notions. Immediate negativity to other ideas and the resultant need to defend one's point of view become accepted as useful and realistic.

A NEW ROLE FOR THE MEETING LEADER

If the purpose of a meeting is to engage and make the utmost use of the people invited, the traditional meeting arrangement must be discarded. Relieved of the burden of self-protection, a member can wholeheartedly devote himself to speculating, imagining, and supporting and considering far-fetched notions—in short, producing the rich variations out of which fresh alternatives and exciting decisions are made.

This may suggest permissiveness and acceptance of irresponsible ideas in the hope of culling a good one. However, the meeting (or managing) problem cannot finally be solved simply by permissiveness, politeness, or irresponsibility; each of these qualities is appropriate and valuable only if properly used. By themselves they are not the answer.

We are here particularly concerned with helping the leader increase his capability of bringing out the best from the members of his group and with helping the individual group member improve his capacity to contribute. We will emphasize the leader's responsibilities, but with the understanding that the Synectics approach is for the whole group to use and cultivate. Recognizing what the leader is trying to do is the foundation of successful participation by each member of the group.

EVERYONE IS IN BUSINESS FOR HIMSELF

While we stress work within meetings, our basic interest is in individuals and how each can function with greater satisfaction to himself. Our research has greatly changed my own view of creativity. I used to think of it as an extraordinary act that produced something new and useful to mankind. I now see it as less cosmic and more common, an everyday affair, a mode of thought and action that is intimately associated with learning and changing not only oneself but one's situation. Though less cosmic, creative behavior matters a little more than anything else, for it is consistent with the deepest purposes of life: to develop and use one's capacities for compassionate accomplishment. An experience will illustrate my thought. Eddie Smith is a fifty-year-old foreman in the stockroom of a large department store. He grew up in a black ghetto and did not graduate from high school. Life was most often something that happened to him. After a course in problem solving we asked him if the course had been useful.

Eddie told us that a trucker who works with him comes in late every day. The boss was going to fire him. Eddie disapproved. He pointed out to the boss the good points of the trucker. He was a willing and dependable worker and easy to get along with. Then he suggested a possible solution: cut a few minutes from the trucker's lunch hour and from his relief time. The boss agreed to keep the trucker on this basis.

Eddie could not describe what had happened to him and it does not matter. He had learned that he could use himself to help the people around him behave in a more appropriate way.

This change in Eddie Smith has enormous implications. The problem-solving course contained no magic. It only helped Eddie realize that he had magical capacities that he was neglecting.

ELEMENTS OF SYNECTICS

Synectics has developed two basic and interrelated approaches: first, procedures that lead to imaginative speculation; second, disciplined ways of behaving so that speculation is not cut down but valued and encouraged.

To increase speculation we concentrate on and magnify the mechanisms you normally use to imagine and speculate. For instance, suppose you are trying to develop a new food product for pets. You are aware that a person identifies, to some extent, with his pet. Your new pet food must therefore appeal first to the owner. You now enter a strange state: you think about things you like, you wonder if the dog would like them too, and you evaluate each idea against what is on the market and various other criteria. "I like steak—so does a dog, but it is too expensive. We could use less expensive cuts, scraps ... but Alpo already has that on the market."

This activity is familiar and has identifiable elements: given the problem you collect data from things you have observed and your own feelings; you form a hypothesis, see how it stands up, modify it if necessary, and evaluate it again. This is the familiar scientific method.

In our experiments we have found that the probability of success is increased if more information is collected. We have developed mechanisms to do this, derived from observing how people naturally work. We exaggerate and separate steps. For instance, when collecting data we enlarge the search area. We not only want market-research facts (an owner buys pet food as though she were going to eat it), we also seek associatory, personal thoughts that may seem irrelevant (I tried dry dog food when I was a kid and it choked me). These seemingly irrelevant facts are difficult to get if asked for directly; our rational training makes them seem silly, and we either forget or do not offer such thoughts. Synectics uses analogy and other indirect means to bring out such apparently irrelevant but potentially valuable facts.

Next, when the time comes for hypothesis formation, we invoke a disciplined way of reacting so that each person is encouraged to make full use of the data in the course of evaluating, modifying, and re-evaluating.

Free speculation and disciplined reaction to it is of urgent importance, for there is a relentless gravity-like force working against speculation. This force is dangerous especially because it is so easily justified as realistic thinking. It is a well-kept secret that people in general (even you and I, and managers in particular) are determined enemies of free speculation. Each of us pays convincing lip service to his willingness—even eagerness—to consider new thoughts and ideas. But a thousand tapes, such as we have made, make liars of us all. People use remarkable ingenuity to make clear by tone, nonverbal slights, tuning out, supposedly helpful criticism, false issues, and outright negativity that they are not only against ideas and change but also against those who propose them. We humans habitually try to protect ourselves *even from our own new ideas.*

It is only because man is, from birth, a creative problem solver of marvelous patience, cunning, and brilliance that we prevail at all over the fear of change that we begin to develop in childhood. These are strong words, but give me a tape of a normal meeting where a group deals with a problem and I will identify supporting evidence for you.

Synectics is a means for consciously penetrating hatred of change and for liberating creative potential that is now only fractionally used. It can increase the probability of using all the talent you have—as leader or group member.

2

The Usual Meeting—
A Study in Frustration

TRADITIONAL PROBLEM-SOLVING MEETINGS

Over the years we have recognized some inadequacies in traditional meetings that are called to solve problems. We have compiled a list of statements that people like yourself have often made about such meetings. This list is not complete, and you may have additional observations of your own.

Our meetings are boring.
My ideas are seldom heard.
Often we don't come to grips with the real problem.
We spend half our time arguing about what the problem is.
It is impossible to solve the problem without speaking openly,
    and you can't do that and survive.
People find fault with every idea.
The people who work for me seem to cooperate, but it later
    appears that they have not really understood.
As a manager, I seem to find that my group depends on me
    for all the ideas.
I am often concerned that I do not get the best from my
    people when I run a meeting.
I often feel that I could run a better meeting than the chair-
    man.
I often feel that I could have done much better on my own.
About half those present don't participate—what a waste of
    time!

Such comments occur at and apply to every level, from board room to project managers—even to unstructured bull sessions between peers.

Early in our research it became apparent that we could discover no perfect way to run a meeting, but we were able to identify a large number of modifications of varied significance that, when tested, seemed to be constructive. Taken together they effected sizable changes in the productivity of these meetings and in the participants' evaluations. These modifications do not *guarantee* success, but they do increase its *probability*. In evaluating the methods we suggest, try to judge by this criterion: Does this reaction, behavior, or procedure increase or decrease the probability of success?

What actually goes on in a typical problem-solving meeting? In the following transcript of a group problem-solving session, we would like you to observe a group in action and try to identify some of the sources of the group's frustration.

This group consisted of five members (the maximum size we use is seven) who first had been given the task not of solving a particular problem, but merely of agreeing, within ten to fifteen minutes, upon a *procedure* for running a meeting to solve a problem. Then they are given an actual problem to solve, hopefully making use of the procedure agreed upon. We have conducted this experiment more than one hundred times, varying the time allowed from thirty minutes to several hours. We have used groups of different composition: a president with his vice presidents, a group leader and his group, and people who had met only minutes before the experiment.

Except for minor differences in politeness (strangers tend to be more polite at first) and in jokes, certain behavioral constants nearly always appear. The transcript that follows is representative of the way most people behave in such a situation. In only one way is it atypical. This group makes no reference at all to their procedure during the actual problem-solving meeting. It is more usual for a group to pay token attention to the procedure now and then.

In their fifteen-minute procedural meeting, the group agreed that when they received the problem they would:

1. Identify and understand the problem.
2. Collect relevant information.
3. Mull it over.
4. Speculate.
5. Develop ideas.
6. Select the best idea.
7. Implement it.

Such step-by-step procedures vary in terminology from group to group, but usually the above steps are represented in some form. Even groups that have been operating regularly together over a long period of time go through much the same process as strangers in articulating and writing up the procedure they intend to follow.

This process is rather interesting in itself. Whenever anyone in a group has recently learned a method such as Kepner-Tregoe[1] or Osborne and Parnes's Brainstorming,[2] he is recognized as an authority, and his version of such a method is accepted. (There is always some verbalized resistance, but not much.) If such a firsthand authority is not present, the dynamics of the meeting change. In our usual groups of five or six people, there are at least two who wish to run the group. They attempt politely and skillfully to take charge of designing the procedure. The result is usually a compromise with qualifications added by other members of the group. In a minority of cases there is enough difference of opinion about process so

[1] Kepner and Tregoe have developed an orderly system for solving problems. Central to their procedure is "specifying the problem." The group identifies very precisely what the problem is and what it is not. See *The Rational Manager*, by Charles H. Kepner and Benjamin B. Tregoe.
[2] Brainstorming is a widely known problem-solving system, the key element of which is the encouragement of wild ideas by postponement of judicial behavior. See *Creative Behavior Guidebook*, by Sidney Parnes.

that no complete procedure is agreed to in the allotted time.

As one is observing this experiment, a number of questions occur, such as: Are *all* members of the group satisfied with the results? Is the plan helpful or restrictive? One way of answering these and other pertinent questions is to ask them directly of the participants. Another way is to see how effectively the group uses the procedure they develop. We shall use both methods.

THERMOS-BOTTLE-CLOSURE PROBLEM

After the fifteen-minute procedural meeting, our groups are given the following problem to solve.

You are familiar with the widemouthed thermos bottle. The mouth is wide to permit the entrance of a spoon for eating stews, etc. Imagine that you have been employed to invent a new closure for this product to replace the plug. The new closure must fall within the following specifications:

> It should be lossproof and integral with the bottle so that the top does not have to be removed to get at the contents. No strings, chains, or hinges.
> Closure must not depend on cup, so that user can reclose bottle while cup is in use.
> The cup top should be retained in some usable form.
> It must not add more than fifty cents to the retail cost.
> It must be easily cleaned.
> It must be thermally effective for ten hours.
> It must hold pressures up to 1½ pounds per square inch.
> No basic change in the thermos bottle itself is acceptable.
> The wide mouth must be retained.

As you follow the transcript of the group's attempt to solve this problem, concentrate on the members' behavior. Focus on the following list of questions, which are meant to serve as a general indicator of the major behavioral issues that we have found important to group effectiveness. For example, question 11 deals with the issue of leadership, whereas questions 1 and 2 deal with the issue of defining the problem. Our discussion of the transcript will involve identifying particular examples of each major behavior issue.

1. Do the group members establish a common understanding of the problem?
2. Do they focus together on a single aspect of the problem, or does each member have his own way of seeing the problem?
3. Do they actually work as a team or as a group of individuals?
4. Do the members take pains to make sure everyone understands each idea?
5. Does anyone use analogies to suggest possible solutions?
6. Do the members *really* listen to one another?
7. Do the members tend to shoot down ideas quickly?

8. Does the group insist that each idea be a complete solution?
9. Or do they support and improve on an unsatisfactory idea?
10. Do they thoroughly explore one idea before going on to the next?
11. What does the group do about leadership?

The meeting took place in a room designed for the purpose. Mounted on one wall are five large easel pads. On two other walls there are wood strips with extending nails on which sheets torn from the pads may be impaled and preserved. There is a microphone visible on the ceiling and cameras so that the proceedings can be tape-recorded and video-taped. There is a couch and three comfortable chairs. (The names of the participants have been changed.) (At first, much fumbling, no talking.)

Paul: I have an image of some kind of balloon, filling it with air, maybe a . . . *(very long pause)* vacuum of air to be blown up every time you want it to close; it puffs up and closes it.

Harry: Do you puff it with your mouth, or does it puff itself up?   5

Paul: Inside . . . I guess maybe when you put your hand   10 there, maybe there would be something inside the thermos bottle that would blow air, but *(laughingly)* maybe then the soup or whatever was inside the thermos bottle would . . . *(laughingly incompleted)*

Harry: Now the problem, it seems, is just to replace this *(holding up stopper),* but in a way that won't come apart.

Paul *(hesitantly):* I don't think so. . . .

Harry: It won't get lost, rather.   15

Al: Yeah, lossproof.

Harry *(reading):* "So the top does not have to be removed." *(Long silence.)*

Rita *(with conviction):* That means it has to be attached; it has to be integral . . . to the . . .

Al *(interrupting)*: Yes, it has to be integral in some   20
way. .... Now this *(holding the cup top)* is to remain unchanged, but this is what we're supposed
to be working on *(holding up stopper)*, isn't that
right?

Group: Yes, I think so. That's what it sounds like, anyway.

Al *(continuing)*: So it doesn't have to incorporate the   25
spoon apparently *(medium pause)* . . . that means
the top *can* be modified . . .

Harry *(to Paul, interrupting Al)*: I think your idea's a   30
good one; let's put it down; let's put down inflation
for one solution.

Paul: OK. *(Another pause.)* Also, the colanders . . .   35
you know the kitchen colanders that come together?
Well, it's the same idea as the cups that you use at
camp that fold up. Maybe you could have something
that could turn and would come out as you turned
it.

Harry: Yeah . . .

Paul: Four or five different ways . . .

Harry *(interrupting)*: Yeah, like that thing on a camera
lens, what do you call it?

Rita: Oh, an iris.   40

Harry: That means that thing, there. . . .

Rita: Uh huh.

Harry: OK. I think that's a good idea.

Paul *(speaking at the same time)*: . . . so that when you   45
twisted it, it would be a . . .

Harry: But tight. This has to be watertight. . . .

Paul: Yes, well this will have to have rubber around the
edges or something.

(Long pause.)

Al: Well, another way, of course, would be springs   50
. . . to flip something shut, or maybe to flip this
thing . . .

Paul: Is that a hinge? *(very politely)* . . . of sorts . . .

Al: A hinge?! No, a hinge would be this *(draws a picture)*.

Paul: I see, and how would the spring . . .

Rita *(forcefully)*: Where would you put a spring? I, uh, uh . . .

Harry: Well, see, he has this iris, and he wants to do   55
like this, and I say you should be able to hold it
back, uh, it should hold back by itself, and when you
close it, it would compress the spring on the latch.
Does that sound right?

Paul: Uh huh, uh huh *(very hesitatingly)*, I think I un-   60
derstand what you mean. . . .

(Long pause.)

Harry: Fill me in on your name again, sir?

John: John Berman.

Al: I usually go by the name of Al—Allard Fairbank.

Paul: Paul.

Rita: Rita.   65

Harry: And I am Harry.

Rita: I am wondering how the iris spring thing is going
to fulfill the specification on being easily cleaned.

Harry: Just by sloshing around in hot water.

Paul: But she means that when it's closed, it's sealed   70
and . . .

Rita: Yeah, it gets all gooked up.

Harry: But you've got soapy water inside. . . .

John *(first time he speaks; forcefully, with some hu-*   75
mor): That's a negative remark! *(Speaking at the*
same time as Harry.)

Harry: Let's not have any negative remarks here until
later. *(Laughter.)* You don't have to evaluate the
solution now.

Rita: Uhhh . . . *(long pause)*.

Al: Does this have to work for both hot and cold ma-   80
terials?

Paul: I gather that's what they mean by a thermos bottle.

Harry: I think it would, yes, because you wouldn't want
just a hot one *(directed to Al)*.

(Long pause.)

John: We could put the cup on the bottom; we could   85
just screw the cup there, so we don't even have to
think about the cup. We could disregard having to
put a cup over the top or whatever. . . .

Harry: That's a good thought, it never occurred to me   90
that we could do that. Then this closure would be
the ultimate, the whole blamed thing and not a
two-piece proposition. . . . *(After a pause):* That
makes it harder, doesn't it? . . .
(Long pause.) Would you think it ought to be flexible
or rubbery or plasticky or something sort of rigid?
John: Let's see. . . . It would have to be at least part   95
flexible; that is, if it didn't have the protection of
the hard top over the flexible closure, then you'd
have to have a . . . some hard part of a . . .
Harry: Something to lend strength.
Paul: Uh huh. *(Pause.)* Well, how do you see it work-   100
ing?
John: I see it as one whole piece, the whole thing. . . .
Paul: The whole unit . . .
John: Yeah, the whole unit as one piece, with the excep-   105
tion of the cup, somehow being able to either by
screwing it, or something . . .
Paul: Like a kaleidoscope!
John: Yeah.
(Pause.)
Harry: Wouldn't it be a whole lot simpler to . . .
Al *(at the same time):* See, there are those hinges. . . .
Harry: Yeah; wouldn't it be almost simpler to have it   110
on some sort of rod, here, like a . . . a . . . coffee-
pot . . . and so . . .
Al: Yeah, but you're gonna have to put a spoon in it
so it'll have to be a lot larger.
Harry: Yeah, well, you know . . . so it's like on a piston   115
arrangement.
Al: Oh, I see, then you won't have to fuss with the
complexity of the top quite as much as before.
Paul: So, it's almost like a regular stopper . . . the rubber
kind . . . only it's on a rod. . . . I see.
Harry: Would that be permanent enough to serve as the   120
ultimate cap without the regular screw top on it?
Al: Well, I'd put the top right back on it!
Harry: I see, you'd say put the existing top right back
on it *(very aggressively).*

Al: Well, you *could;* in other words, I think in this case 125
that's sort of irrelevant to the solution of the closure problem.

John: I don't know if that meets all of the qualifications
or not. . . .

Harry: Well, even if it doesn't, let's not eliminate it 130
(writes on board). Must the top remain circular?

Group: No. Well, it doesn't say so.

Harry: Does that do anything for us if it were not circular?

Paul: I have a feeling that if it has corners it will be very
difficult to clean.

Harry: Well, maybe elongated . . . 135

Paul: Or elliptical.

Rita: How about a slide-on cap?

Harry: Well, let's see, there's to be no basic change in
the thermos bottle. I guess we've got to keep that
in mind.

Al: Well, couldn't you have a . . . 140

Rita: You could have a rectangular slide-on that . . .
that . . .

Harry *(interrupting):* Yeah, yeah . . . fits into a little
shaft here *(back to his rod idea?)* and slips right on.

Rita: Oh, I think that would be awful. . . .

Al *(ignoring her):* Yeah, I think that's a good thought; 145
or like the top of a spice . . .

Paul: It might not have a flat bottom.

Al *(at the same time as Paul):* This might mean a basic
change in the bottle, however.

Paul *(again, louder):* It might not have a flat bottom!

Al: Yeah, are we violating that basic qualification? I 150
suppose we are.

Paul *(feeling guilty?):* I don't think it's so basic. I mean
it's an external change.

Harry *(goes into a long dissertation about the construc-* 155
tion of the thermos and ends up on the subject of
insulation): Now, this iris device, we're going to
need some sort of insulation for it to be very good.

Paul: Yeah . . . yeah . . . I don't know what to do
about it.

Rita: What sort of insulation is in the regular thermos?

Harry: I don't know, some sort of Styrofoam or some- 160
thing like that.

Rita: Well, couldn't you have a thick rubber iris with
some sort of Styrofoam inside it or something like
that?

Al: How flexible would that be?

Harry *(at the same time):* Yeah, I suppose you could. 165

Rita: I am not so sure about cleaning it *(shoots down
own idea). (The group then works on the piston
idea, which starts to take shape. Then . . .)*

Paul: That's a very good idea, but somehow I see a 170
piece of stew right over there.

Harry: So do I.

Paul *(laughingly):* . . . and getting stuck.

Harry: And what's going to stop it from coming right
on up?

Al: Oh, at some point or other there'll be a hold on it 175
somewhere inside. But the whole thing would be
flexible, with on part sliding inside the other.

Harry: Oh, yes, I see *(cutting him off.)* How does that
sound to the rest of you?

(Short pause.)

Rita: It seems impossible to clean . . . at the risk of being 180
terribly negative again.

Harry *(picks up Rita's complaint, continues as she also
speaks):* Yes, it does seem like food would get
caught between the flanges and it would be impossible to clean. . . .

Like the members of the group itself, you may have
felt that it was a good meeting: some good ideas were
considered, and everyone seemed generally cordial and
helpful. As we mentioned earlier, people have been conditioned to think and act critically and to accept criticism
for bad ideas—so long as it is done nicely and with a
minimum of personal reference. Consequently, they tend
to suppress their hostile reactions, to cover them up with
humor, or to withdraw from the conversation, unless, of

course, they actually do come out and shout another person down. In the preceding transcript, the usual reactions were in evidence, and they took their toll on the group's efforts. There were also constructive reactions that helped develop potentially good ideas. The tragedy is that the proportion of damaging behaviors is so high when people do what comes naturally.

In evaluating a meeting one is tempted to generalize, to think of the over-all meeting and its results and say, "That was a pretty good meeting," or "That was a poor meeting." We have found it more useful to identify a specific, take it out of context, and make a tentative decision about its value. For example, one member interrupts another with his own idea and later invites the member to return to discussing the prior idea. We consider the interruption, the discussion of the new idea, and the invitation to return to the prior idea as three specific behaviors, each with its own consequences.

In analyzing this transcript we are going to draw conclusions that may seem too far-reaching for the evidence at hand. These conclusions are based on examinations of hundreds of similar situations. When you question one of our assumptions, weigh it according to the criterion we have constantly used: "Does this behavior increase the probability of success or decrease it?"

In the very first remark in the session, Paul offers the beginnings of an idea: "I have an image of some kind of balloon." This is a common phenomenon. When a person is faced with a problem, his natural reaction is to think in terms of a solution. Predetermined procedures, such as the plan developed by this group, nearly always get pushed aside whenever a possible solution occurs to any member of the group. We say possible solution because most innovative ideas come out in embryonic form. It is up to the individuals in the group to build the new idea—to help it grow, take form, and become strong.

Unfortunately, however, our analytic training and our competitive upbringing make us search instead for the weaknesses of the idea, to find out *why* the new idea won't work rather than *how* we can make it work. This is the reaction to Paul's first suggestion; Harry chooses to ignore the general concept of a balloon-like closure and focuses on the specific details of Paul's invention. He challenges Paul to give him detailed specifications, but Paul is in no position to answer because he has not had time to think it through, and perhaps he does not really know how to do it anyway. Paul is thus pressed to *prove* that his idea is good by showing exactly how it would work. In such a situation, a person naturally tends to feel defensive and to accept the challenge, at least temporarily. Paul tries to defend his idea but then retreats and dismisses it by making a joke of it. Laughter probably helped to ease the pain, but the damage had been done. When questioned later, Harry of course denied putting Paul on the spot; he was interested only "in getting a better idea of what Paul had in mind." That probably was his conscious motive, but what is of major consequence to them, and to us, is the *effect* of his action—on Paul, on the rest of the group, and on the idea under discussion. Perhaps he did not *mean* to antagonize Paul; possibly he thought the idea basically a good one. But the effect of his question was to reduce the probability of developing a solution from Paul's germ of an idea.

When this point comes up participants quite often say, "I find such questioning stimulating. It makes me work harder to overcome the objections that are raised." This may be valid for some people. However, in nearly all the cases we have observed, newborn half ideas tend not to survive this type of treatment.

After Harry has disposed of Paul, he continues in what we see as his bid for leadership and control of the group. He gives a statement of the problem—*his* statement of the problem, presented as if it were *the* statement of the problem—and later he backs it up by a quotation from the specifications (line 17). The natural reaction to such an assertion, when others view the problem differently, is some sort of challenge. This time, as one might have predicted, the challenge comes from Paul. He does not offer an alternative interpretation—he simply says, "I don't think so." We suspect he is reacting to Harry's previous treatment. But the crucial issues at stake here concern *definition* of the problem to be solved: how it is defined, who defines it, and what to do about multiple definitions. Let us recall some of the questions we raised earlier.

> Do the group members establish a common understanding of the problem?
> Do they focus together on a single aspect of the problem, or does each member have his own way of seeing the problem?

In our experience each individual will have his own unique way of seeing the problem even if that way is in basic agreement with that of a teammate. Unless there is an articulated agreement by the group concerning what particular approach they are going to take to the problem, there is confusion, because everyone works in his own, exclusive framework. For example, Harry may see the problem as one of trying to build a better stopper, while Rita may be trying to invent an integral closure. Al may be trying to invent a stopper that is lossproof. Certainly there is much overlap among these individual approaches, but they are different enough so that a solution to one might run afoul of the restrictions of another.

There is more difficulty. If Al operates in his frame of reference and Harry voices a thought from *his*, there is a strong tendency for Al to listen for a moment, decide Harry's thought is not relevant, and tune him out. The result is that what looks promising to one person may not only be unacceptable to another, it may not even be heard.

Another complication involving statements of the problem concerns *whose* approach should be the one the group uses. The implied assumption here—that the group is *aware* that different ways of seeing the problem do exist and do interfere—is quite a large assumption that isn't usually supported by group actions. People don't always realize that they see the problem differently from others, and when they do, they are reluctant to give up their personal approaches; this is natural, because their own viewpoints make the most sense to them. But let us suppose that there *is* recognition of the need for a single, group approach; how then does the selection of such an approach take place? This introduces the issue of group leadership.

Our experience has shown us that in every group of five or six people, two or three vie for the position of leadership. Usually, the person who is most successful in asserting his approach to the problem gets temporary control. But he finds it necessary to protect his position from repeated challenges by the others. These are seldom overt bids for power that might bring the leadership struggle into the open; people have learned oblique and subtle ways to wrest control from the incumbent. Al, beginning in line 20, holds up a piece of the problem (the cup top), restates the problem, and asks the group to support him in power: ". . . isn't that right?" Group: "Yes." And Al is off and running—at least until the next challenge.

In a structured group with a chairman or a vice president, these challenges are carefully executed within polite, accepted contexts: the pointed question, the show of expertise. The methods are varied and clever. The assumption that a meeting with structure will therefore be efficient is open to question. We have observed and taped many seemingly well-run traditional meetings. Evidence of sabotage, revenge, and power seeking has always been there. One result is that a great deal of energy which should be used in working toward a solution is expended in subtle personal rivalry.

Let us go back to the dialogue: Harry reads from the text to support his position ("So the top does not have to be removed"). There is a long silence, broken only by a challenge to his dominance by Rita (line 18), whose challenge is then interrupted by Al. Al gets tentative group support, so he further defines *his* approach to the problem ("So it doesn't have to incorporate the spoon apparently . . . that means the top *can* be modified"). Harry (to Paul): "I think your idea's a good one; let's put it down . . ."). This may seem innocent until you have listened to it happen many times and discussed it openly with perceptive Harrys. Harry is aware that Al is a competitor for leadership and that he is winning. So Harry tunes Al out and directs the group's attention to Paul's balloon. Paul responds to this apparent support with still another idea: a telescoping colander (lines 32 to 35). Harry *(interrupting):* "Yeah, like that thing on a camera lens, what do you call it?"

Again, this behavior may seem innocent enough until it has been repeatedly observed in groups and investigated. Then you realize that Harry has only half heard Paul. He feigns agreement to get an opening so he can introduce an entirely different idea. In post-mortem discussion, a person like Harry, with some support (seldom from a person like Paul), will say, "I heard Paul, and it gave me this idea. This is really what this is all about, isn't it—to use other people's thoughts to help evoke better ideas?"

This *is* what meetings are all about. However, by introducing the camera lens while Paul had a half-formed idea before the group, Harry prevented the development of an idea potentially as good as his own.

We must also ask whether Harry really heard *and understood* what Paul was saying. In the post-mortem Harry usually cannot reconstruct what Paul had in mind. This raises another basic issue: listening. When group members often fail to hear each other, it damages the probability of success in serious respects. It causes resentment, either conscious or subconscious (Paul remembers later quite clearly how his colander idea was treated). It encourages every-man-for-himself reactions. Ideas fail to be developed. Opportunities are missed.

Sometimes members are aware that they have been ignored and merely try harder to assert themselves, whereas others may tend to withdraw resentfully from group activity. *Listening* to another person's point of view is perhaps the single most important aspect of Synectics training. We shall have a more complete discussion of it later.

We have found that a responsive group atmosphere is critical to creative productivity. If this response is negative, it will greatly reduce the probability of having a successful problem-solving venture. By a negative response, we mean much more than "It won't work because . . ." As you can see in the brief transcript above, there are many other ways to show hostility to an idea. Some may even seem polite: "That is an excellent idea but . . ." Flattery, politeness, and insincere support are quickly spotted. The most sensitive detector of manipulative behavior or lack of candor is the group member himself. Yet in spite of this sensitivity and awareness, a person often chooses to accept superficially polite responses because it is the custom: "We are all grown-up, mature people."

Even neutral or nonsupportive responses can be damaging. If one member thinks he has the start of a good idea, but he does not know how to finish it, it is extremely important that his suggestion be met with an active, *honest* show of support, even if no one can make a positive suggestion. Just saying, "I like your idea, let's see how we can get over this one snag," can make a world of difference. Such a response is much more helpful than sitting quietly by while a thought and its creator dangle in mid-air. Silence, then, can be a form of negativity, interpreted by the individual as a snub or as a challenge to support himself. Far too frequently his reaction will be the same when a teammate is in trouble: "He didn't help me, so why should I help him?" Again it is *probability* of success that suffers.

In the transcript Rita is able to help Harry: "Oh, an iris," and the idea receives attention and help until Harry himself seems to find a snag. "But tight. This has to be watertight," and the idea is killed instantly. This attack is followed by a *very* long pause—members become even more reluctant to verbalize ideas that are incomplete.

Al then introduces an idea quite different from the iris (line 47). "Well, another way, of course, would be springs." Paul: "Is that a hinge?" Can you guess the motive behind that polite question? Does Paul or anyone else know exactly what Al has in mind? The tone of Al's reply, lost in the written words, was basically one of, "No, stupid, *this* is a hinge." The idea withstands the familiar abuses for another minute or so, but then succumbs to the one reaction that can kill most ideas: skillful diversion. While Al's idea is still only half expressed and half considered, Harry suddenly asks everyone's name. The first person he asks has not yet made any contribution to the session. We suspect Harry is trying to regain control as leader. At any rate, the discussion is interrupted. It resumes with Rita's statement: "I am wondering how the iris spring thing is going to fulfill the specification on being easily cleaned" (line 67). Let's examine this statement.

Rita is questioning the usefulness of the whole idea by drawing attention to one shortcoming. Harry defends his idea with, "Just by sloshing around in hot water," but Paul joins the attack on the iris spring: "But she means that when it's closed, it's sealed and . . ." Rita: "Yeah, it gets all gooked up."

Another point that should be raised is how much women are allowed to contribute to a meeting of this kind. It was fairly obvious in the above transcript that Rita, al-though for the most part negative to others' ideas, did have suggestions to make which may have led to a new way of attacking the problem. As mentioned earlier, she is skeptical about the spring idea (line 54) and is con-cerned about fulfilling the specifications on being easily cleaned. However, when she did suggest a new approach, "How about a slide-on cap? (line 137), Harry's immedi-ate reaction was, in effect, "Didn't you even bother to read the specifications, woman? There's to be no basic change in the thermos bottle." He was using his interpre-tation of the specifications to tell her she was wasting her time thinking in a new direction. Again, Rita tries to ex-plain to the group what she has in mind, and immediately Harry interrupts her in order to focus attention on his old "rod" idea. Rita gets her revenge. "Oh, I think that would be awful."

Although not all men act as overtly as Harry, we have frequently observed that men tend to take women's sug-gestions less seriously than those of other men. This is particularly true with technological problems, but it is by no means limited to this field. By slighting women in this way, men frequently miss the fresh new approaches that sometimes only strangers can bring to bear on an overworked problem. Experts, in particular, must be care-ful not to prejudge women's capabilities and the potential value of their contributions.

In summary, we have noticed that polite behavior can frequently mask hostility that effectively kills a poten-tially good idea. One of the primary causes of this is our rigid analytical training, which makes us feel that the only good idea is a perfect idea—that only ideas presented in final, acceptable form are worthy of exploration. As a result, unformed ideas with possible potential never receive the energy necessary to build them to greatness. This artificial insistence on completeness all too often means that the only ideas which are really considered are the superficial ones—those which can be quickly completed and made defensible. Such defense-oriented thinking relies heavily on the already known and already accepted, and it works against speculation with the half-known or unknown intuitive thought. This prevents the emergence of fresh, innovative, daring ideas.

One result of the treatment given to incomplete ideas in traditional group meetings is that many good thinkers, because of their unfortunate experiences when they speculate, tend to avoid group work; meetings for them are for doodling or for political maneuvering and not for real problem solving. These people at least continue to speculate on their own. A different effect that is even more corrosive to the individual and corporate good is that speculation is perceived as a dangerous and unwelcome activity. Policy seems to say: stamp it out.

As a result of this and other experiences, most of us are as destructive toward our own ideas and intuitions as we are toward those of others. The same patterns of thinking that interfere with group productivity also interfere with individual productivity. This can be as destructive as any group behavior.

It is virtually impossible for the individuals in a group to agree on a single approach to a particular problem. But our urge toward reaching consensus is so strong that we pretend to reach it. People ordinarily assume that they are all working on the same aspect of a problem, when at times they most definitely are not. This confusion reinforces people's tendency to withhold ideas which do not seem to fit the varied and unspoken requirements of the individual group members.

Furthermore, people fail to see any value in others' ideas when these ideas are inconsistent with their own thoughts. This is one symptom of the problem of poor listening which we mentioned earlier.

Finally, there is rivalry concerning leadership. People seem to resent leaders, and the rivalry diverts energy from the meeting's stated goal. Leadership is a problem that can reduce the participation and involvement of the individual members.

A NEW CONCEPT OF WORK

Negativity, rigidity, confusion, and competitiveness are major issues that we must deal with if we are to increase the probability of success in problem solving. The pervasive presence of these four behaviors not only in meetings but also within most of our institutions for education and accomplishment is tragic. There are tools to fashion a better way. Some are described in this book. These, combined with some of the lessons taught in Sensitivity Training,[3] Organization Development,[4] Encounter Groups,[5] and other systems, are enough for a start. All that is needed now is the courage and persistence to experiment and adapt at every level.

Working with a highly productive group is an exciting experience. Whenever we observe such a group, we find deliberately constructive behavior. As for the more usual, less productive groups, we do not believe that the members set out consciously to behave destructively; people lack models or rules for teamwork in a meeting. Everyone assumes that from family, school, and business he has learned how to behave effectively and constructively. If

[3] Sensitivity Training is a procedure aimed at first developing awareness of the effect of one's own behavior on other people and then devising better modes for communicating with others. See *T-Group Theory and Laboratory Method*, by Leland P. Bradford, J. R. Gibb, and K. D. Benne.

[4] Organization Development is a system for improving operations within a company by repeatedly examining the processes used to get things done. See *The Managerial Grid*, by R. R. Blake and J. S. Mouton.

[5] "Encounter Groups" is a term used to describe various experiments aimed at helping individuals derive joy from themselves and from their relationships with other people. See *Joy: Expanding Human Awareness*, by William C. Schutz.

you examine the lessons taught by family, school, or business, a degree of cooperation with others *is* learned and verbally emphasized; however, judging from thousands of observations, the most basic and overwhelming lesson is: compete, watch out for number one, and do it politely, if possible.

Our concern is to discover ways to promote constructive *behavior* changes that are consistent with individual needs. We have concentrated our attention on behaviors because they can be observed while attitudes cannot. From experiments we know that by changing the behaviors of only two out of six members of a group, we can markedly change how everyone in the group perceives how they are doing. We are convinced that by modifying behaviors a group can greatly increase its probability of success.

One method of changing behavior is to point out destructive reactions. This is moderately useful in teaching, but its greatest value comes when the group, knowing how each member should behave, reminds a member who forgets.

The great difficulty in changing derives from the fact that most destructive behavior is habitual, unconscious, and probably unintentional. It may even be viewed as *unavoidable* in the context of traditional problem-solving meetings. Because habit is strong and tradition blinds, we knew that we must devise a system or policy that has built-in reinforcement; one that would somehow demand that group members actively honor and use each other's capacities. It seemed essential also to create a situation in which each member welcomed the opportunity to give as much as he is able. This has implications of unselfishness that we do not intend. Our view is that to ask a person to involve himself in activities that do not demonstrably (to him) serve his own highly personal needs is to invite token participation.

This view has far-reaching significance. In our work with industry, education, and the church, we have been exposed mainly to upper-level innovators: research-and-development scientists, teachers, ministers, and managers of all sorts. Theirs is considered by many to be the most rewarding kind of work. Yet we are impressed with the widespread boredom (a symptom of serious trouble) and tokenism found among them, for their boredom suggests that workers at the more routine levels are even more bored. In far too many jobs and positions there is, as the coal miner says, "hardly enough to keep the mind alive."[6]

We believe the top management that rethinks the work assignments from manager to production-line worker will reap enormous rewards. It will need the active help of those involved (the production worker is the expert on that particular form of boredom) and much creative behavior to design into each job some continuing form of personal achievement and satisfaction.

But instant revolution is not necessary. For example, if one re-examines the role of a supervisor with an open mind and respect for persons, it requires only a slight change of focus to see him as primarily a teacher. Since he teaches subordinates how to accomplish tasks he must learn from them what impedes them. Thus the supervisor is a teacher-learner. His subordinate is the same. This makes clear the actual dependence each has on the other. If pursued, this could lead to a more realistic and enjoyable relationship than the present one, which focuses on rank and authority.

[6] *Beyond the Fringe,* a satirical review by Alan Bennett, Peter Cooke, Jonathan Miller, and Dudley Moore (New York: Random House, 1963).

3

New Structure, New Roles

As described in that classic model *Robert's Rules of Order*, meetings are designed to keep order and allow conflicting views to be stated and supported. Nearly all chairmen we have observed in our research use a casual, personal fusion of *Robert's Rules*, legal, military, and Dale Carnegie models. We believe that this approach prejudices the outcome toward mediocrity. As you saw in the thermos meeting, random behavior, which this potluck leadership produces, tends to be careless of the ideas and feelings of others. And surprisingly, when a person is careless toward others it is highly probable that he is also careless and negative toward his own ideas and feelings.

To redirect the energies in a meeting you need a new model to guide your behavior as chairman or leader. A good model is like a new set of nerve endings. When proceedings go wrong, you get signals. Ideally you see what is wrong and you know how to set it right. But to avoid overcontrol, your model should be as simple and economical as a lever.

Possibly your most important activity is clarification. You must constantly be aware of purposes and forces. To do this you must understand them yourself.

The most important, most powerful, and most delicate force at your disposal is the mind of each member of your group. In a meeting, these minds work so skillfully and so speedily that they are prone to distract and hinder each other unless you set context, style, and purpose.

First, assume that every meeting is for problem solving. This may clarify your own thinking about meetings. My bias is that minds in a group are such a powerful and precious force that they should never be wasted. A lecture is an invitation to develop a bad habit—uninvolved boredom. For example, information meetings are inexcusably wasteful. If exchange is desirable, publish it and have a meeting for questions and answers. Even better, have a meeting to solve a problem involving the information. If you want people to know about your pension plan, invite them to a meeting where they try to define the problems that the pension plan should solve. Your pension expert serves as a resource.

In traditional meetings involvement, like too many other aspects, is left to chance. Obtaining full participation among all the members is mainly the chairman's responsibility, and to properly fulfill it he must know how and when to use his power. When you are chairman a two-level model is useful. At one level you want to know the step-by-step procedure you would like to have happen. At the other, more emotional level, you must keep the sensitivity and aggression on the problem, not on personalities.

If we look through the emotional fog of the usual meeting we can see two kinds of activity. *Understanding* the problem and *solving* it. Understanding consists of (a) getting a personal feel for some of the elements of the problem and (b) then imagining or dreaming a possible solution. For instance, suppose the problem concerns automobile seat belts. Most people do not fasten them. It is easy for me to have a personal interest in this problem because I have seat belts and often fail to fasten them. Next I imagine a solution: have the seat belts fasten themselves.

With that, I have completed one understanding cycle. Now I move to solving. I search my mind for a way to make a seat belt fasten itself. I think of the mechanical arm that handles radioactive materials remote from the person. I suggest one of those for each person. Now I (or an expert) test this against reality. It could work but it would be too expensive, bulky, hard, etc. Now I have completed one solving cycle. I have a new and better understanding of the problem. My possible or dream solution—a belt that fastens itself—is still good, but I must search for a better way to do it.

Every aspect of these activities is creative. These steps happen very fast and they recycle. Human beings are, before anything else, programed to solve their problems. I believe that this is the way learning happens. We are all naturally skillful and creative at problem solving. Bad habits of unnecessary precision, censorship, and anxiety about the regard of others have made nearly all of us largely ignorant of our own capabilities. "The human animal is the only one on earth so intelligent that it can actually learn to be stupid."[1]

This inherent problem-solving capacity is, tragically, the best-kept secret of our age.

As chairman of a meeting you must be aware of each of these activities so you can encourage them and differentiate the behavioral activities that will dissipate energy and confuse purposes. The opportunities for misdirection are endless. To be constructive requires not only that you be alert but also that you develop a technique and an *intent* that will help you use seeming distractions for the good in them. For example, a typical sequence in a meeting about the seat-belt problem would be:

Jim: How about a seat belt that fastens itself?
Joe: That doesn't really solve the problem. Isn't the basic problem one of safety? The seat belt is only part of the answer.

A chairman with the proper models and a good ear might insert his lever between Jim and Joe like this:

[1] Siegfried and Therese Engelmann, *Give Your Child. a Superior Mind*, p. 59.

Chair: Joe, it seems to me Jim's idea would solve an important part of the problem if we can figure a way to do it. *(You must protect Jim and his way of thinking from the need to defend.)* You are right, too, about safety being the over-all problem. *(You don't devaluate Joe and his thinking.)* Will you think of a way of describing your goal—total safety—while we pursue Jim's idea?

You know that both Joe and Jim are understanding the problems by imagining a solution or possible resolution. An argument about whether the problem has to do with seat belts or safety is worse than useless. Each person needs to understand in his own individual way. This fact illuminates a widespread, damaging myth about problem-solving meetings: you must have consensus about the problem. Many man-years are wasted daily on trying to get agreement about the problem to be worked on. Consensus is impossible and even undesirable in the understanding of most problems. You will see later how we handle this seeming paradox.

The step-by-step meeting model is simple. The behavioral model of a meeting is not. Each person has a wonderfully varied repertoire of responses and reactions. Fortunately, given an understanding of basic concerns and premises, nearly anyone can learn to lead a group into productive behavior.

Sensitivity and aggressiveness were necessary to our survival and progress in the distant past. They remain powerful motivators in the present. Misunderstood and misdirected, these capacities can destroy us. In a problem-solving meeting the leader must have a solid understanding of how and why sensitivity and aggression are habitually misused as competitive weapons in order to recognize and redirect. There are two elements that govern our behavioral model. First, each member perceives a meeting as a contest, a competition. He sees himself, to some degree, losing if another person is winning. Second he carries into the meeting with him a delicate image of himself. It is easily damaged by any slight, slur, or put-down of his thinking. If and when this happens, he loses interest in everything but repairing the damage.

Perhaps the most remarkable lesson that has emerged from our work is the fact that people cannot whole-heartedly work in a group unless the individuality of each is carefully protected.

In summary, an effective meeting model will take into account the two problem-solving activities: understanding and solving. It will provide for protection of each member's sensitivity and direction for his aggressiveness. It will recognize that a meeting between two or more people is perceived, to some degree, as a personal win-lose contest in which one is, from past experience, vulnerable.

In a later chapter we will deal with a variety of step-by-step procedures. Compared to the behavioral difficulties in a meeting, however, these procedures are relatively unimportant.

LISTENING

We have mentioned good listening as perhaps the single most important aspect of Synectics training. The kind of listening we have in mind is both a skill and an attitude. It is crucial to meaningful communication between individuals. Unfortunately good listening is not highly valued in our culture and, like effective speaking, must be learned. To become a good listener one must not only learn the rules but must also practice continually.

Most of our behavioral models, such as parents and teachers, are typically bad listeners. Listening is usually seen as trying to figure out as quickly as possible what is the gist of another person's message. This gist is carefully screened by the listener's preconceptions. The listener then tunes out and prepares his own official statement on the subject he assumes is under discussion. Once you have become a skilled listener, you will observe that it is more the rule than the exception that people talk *at* one another rather than *with* one another. Each person may make telling and cogent points, but this doesn't necessarily constitute an actual discussion. People often seem to talk just for the sake of hearing themselves speak, with no attempt to carry on real communication. In the example below, no one seems to be concerned with what the other person is saying or whether his own thoughts are being heard.

A. What do you think about the traffic problem here in Cambridge? Terrible, isn't it?

B. You can say that again! I still haven't learned which streets are one-way and which aren't.

C. I know what you mean. It's getting so it's not worth it to drive to work; you can spend all day finding a parking place.

A. Not only that but they crack down immediately. Even if you go down a one-way street the wrong way on the very first day!

The clinical psychologist Carl Rogers investigated the role of poor listening as a communication block. He says,

I would like to propose, as an hypothesis for consideration, that the major barrier to mutual interpersonal communication is our very natural tendency to judge, to evaluate, to approve or disapprove, the statement of the other person, or the other group. Let me illustrate my meaning with some very simple examples. As you leave the meeting tonight, one of the statements you are likely to hear is, "I didn't like that man's talk." Now what do you respond? Almost invariably your reply will be either approval or disapproval of the attitude expressed. Either you respond, "I didn't either. I thought it was terrible," or else you tend to reply, "Oh, I thought it was really good." In other words, your primary reaction is to evaluate what has just been said to you, to evaluate it from *your* point of view, your own frame of reference.[2]

[2] Carl R. Rogers, "Communication: Its Blocking and Its Facilitation."

Rogers then describes a more emotional encounter in which there is even less communication. Then he adds:

The tendency to react to any emotionally meaningful statement by forming an evaluation of it from our own point of view, is, I repeat, *the major barrier to interpersonal communication* [italics added]. But is there any way of solving this problem of avoiding this barrier? I feel that we are making exciting progress toward this goal and I would like to present it as simply as I can. Real communication occurs, and this evaluative tendency is avoided, when we listen with understanding. What does that mean? It means to see the expressed idea and attitude from the other person's point of view, to sense how it feels to him, to achieve his frame of reference in regard to the thing he is talking about.

Some of you may be feeling that you listen well to people, and that you have never seen . . . results. The chances are very great indeed that your listening has not been of the type I have described. Fortunately I can suggest a . . . laboratory experiment which you can try to test the quality of your understanding. The next time you get into an argument with your wife, or your friend, or with a small group of friends, just stop the discussion for a moment and for an experiment, institute this rule. "Each person can speak up for himself only *after* he has first restated the ideas and feelings of the previous speaker accurately, and to that speaker's satisfaction." You see what this would mean. It would . . . mean that before presenting your own point of view, it would be necessary for you to really achieve the other speaker's frame of reference—to understand his thoughts and feelings so well that you could summarize them for him. Sounds simple, doesn't it? But if you try it you will discover it one of the most difficult things you have ever tried to do. However, once you have been able to see the other's point of view, your own comments will have to be drastically revised. You will also find the emotion going out of the discussion, the differences being reduced, and those differences which remain being of a rational and understandable sort.

Dr. Rogers tells us further of a deeply rooted difficulty which everyone must deal with if he wants to learn to listen effectively:

In the first place it takes courage, a quality which is not too widespread. . . . If you really understand another person in this way, if you are willing to enter his private world and see the way [a thought or an idea] appears to him, without any attempt to make evaluative judgments, you run the risk of being changed yourself. You might see it his way, you might find yourself influenced in your attitudes or your personality. This risk of being changed is one of the most frightening prospects most of us can face. . . . [If we had to listen to a speech by Senator Joe McCarthy or Mao Tse-tung] how many of us would dare to try to see the world from each of these points of view? The great majority of us could not *listen;* we would find ourselves compelled to *evaluate,* because listening would seem too dangerous. So the first requirement is courage, and we do not always have it.

I have said that our research and experience to date would make it appear that breakdowns in communication, and the evaluative tendency which is the major barrier to communication, can be avoided. The solution is provided by creating a situation in which each of the different parties comes to understand the other from the *other's* point of view. This has been achieved, in practice, even when feelings run high, by the influence of a person who is willing to understand each point of view empathically, and who thus acts as a catalyst to precipitate further understanding. This procedure has important characteristics. It can be initiated by one party, without waiting for the other to be ready. It can even be initiated by a neutral third person, providing he can gain a minimum of cooperation from one of the parties. This procedure can deal with the insincerities, the defensive exaggerations, the lies, the "false fronts" which characterize almost every failure in communication. These defensive distortions drop away with astonishing speed as people find that the only intent is to understand, not judge. This approach leads steadily and rapidly toward the discovery of the truth, toward a realistic appraisal of the objective barriers to communication. The dropping of some defensiveness by one party leads to further dropping of defensiveness by the other party, and the truth is thus approached. This procedure gradually achieves mutual communication. Mutual communication tends to be pointed toward solving a problem rather than toward attacking a person or group. It leads to a situation in which I see how the problem appears to you, as well as to me, and you see how it appears to me, as well as to you. Thus accurately and realistically defined, the problem is almost certain to yield to intelligent attack, or if it is in part insoluble, it will be comfortably accepted as such.

We have applied Dr. Rogers' work on mutual listening to our problem-solving situations. One way in which good listening has proved especially useful is in the early stages of a developing solution. In this case, good listening means setting aside your usual critical, analytical urges and trying to get in your mind a full picture of the new idea with all its rich ambiguities and incompleteness. This demanding activity requires that you lend your mind to your teammates. Because their message may not always be expressed verbally or completely, it is frequently necessary to get behind the spoken words. Behind these first, hesitant words lie intentions, feelings, intuitions—even hopes. These often prove to be the most important forces behind the beginning of an innovative idea. We try to view these as opportunities, chances for you to reach into your own disparate knowledge and experience, to add something to strengthen the new idea; chances, perhaps, even to go beyond what has been said and to see possibilities that have been felt, but not articulated.

As you learn to listen and to be responsive to what another person means and as you discover how to leash your negative reactions temporarily, you find that life is more interesting because you are expanding the areas that mean something to you. By holding in abeyance your negative concerns about a new idea, you release a neglected capacity to contribute, to advance, to add to the creative sum of an emerging idea. This is the stuff of which satisfaction is made.

THE SPECTRUM POLICY

Changing these restrictive habits is not easy. To help, we have devised some rather mechanistic means. Here, for example, is a way of viewing an idea. The statement of an idea includes or implies a spectrum. When you hear the idea, a picture or representation forms in your mind. Parts of what you see may be unacceptable. In the thermos problem, blowing up a balloon and using it as a stopper not only does not meet the specifications (loss-proof); it has immediate problems of durability, convenience, sealing, etc. At the more acceptable end of the spectrum, however, it might indeed form a stopper; it could collapse and take up no space; and it has dead air that would help with the insulation problem. The point here is that this suggestion is not a complete solution but it is not a bad beginning. Most statements share this characteristic: some aspects seem bad in that they raise specters of trouble; other aspects are good in that they help solve parts of the problem.

Our analytical training and our competitive habits too often trap us into taking a black-or-white position: "That won't work because . . ." or, more politely but fooling no one (except, possibly, yourself), "That is a good idea, but . . ." and rarely, "That is a good idea because. . . ." Black-or-white thinking is simply a bad habit, and bad habits can be broken. For practice, try looking at an idea or suggestions as a spectrum.

As we observed in the transcript, people focus on and discuss the bad area of the spectrum. This is natural because the bad elements loom threateningly in the forefront of your mind. But when you indulge this natural tendency, you pay a large price in teamwork, in involvement, and in probability of developing solutions. People protest that it is unrealistic and a waste of time to pursue an idea that has fatal flaws. We agree, but we have repeatedly observed that in the early stages of an emerging idea no one can know with certainty that a flaw is in fact fatal. It seems to be universal that the faults in an idea will take precedence in your mind, so don't fight it; simply do not voice the faults. Comfort yourself with the silent promise that you will get to them in good time. Then temporarily focus the very best of you—your intellect, your feelings, your intuitions—on that small portion of the idea that is worthwhile. Talk about it.

> Harry: I like your balloon idea. . . . It could deflate and get out of the way for the spoon . . . and the air in the balloon when it's blown up—that dead air is a good insulator.

Now you have earned the right to bring out the faults, but choose your words not to prove a negative point but rather to seek help in finding a solution. Cure the faults if you are able.

> Harry: I am concerned about how easy it is to puncture a balloon . . . a fork . . . But if we used a heavy-gauge material, that would take care of that problem. How could we make that heavy balloon lossproof? And convenient?

At this point, it might be helpful to look back at the relevant part of the transcript, putting yourself in Paul's shoes. Would constructive treatment of the idea put more heart in you and lead you to more effort?

To practice the Spectrum Method with effectiveness, you must first hear and understand an idea. When people are learning to use the Spectrum Policy on their own problems, we often see an early reaction of consternation and sealed lips: "I can't see *anything* good in what Paul is saying." In such cases, we suggest that they ask Paul to keep talking about his notion while they try to hear something good. We believe that the good is there but is difficult to hear because of the interference caused by awareness of the faults. As you become skillful you will find that there really is good intent in every suggestion. You will be able to hear it, pick it up, and use it. By reacting this way you promote a speculative discussion that can build rather than an airing of different points of view that invites defensiveness and deadlock.

For example, in a discussion about crime Mr. A says, "I would put a policeman on every block and enforce the letter of the law." Mr. B considers the implications of this and replies, "I like the idea of someone on every block. That level of attention and care will make a lot of people feel protected. The guards or whatever we call them could have two-way radios, too, and that could be an early-warning system. My concern is the connotation of force that seems likely to cause trouble. How can we get the security without that?" Mr. C: "With the same sort of investment—perhaps less—we could get each block or neighborhood to organize its own crime-prevention system. Who could sponsor it other than the police?"

In another case a parent-and-teacher group is working on the drug problem in their high school. Mrs. D: "I am convinced that talking about this is not enough. Every parent should be part of the enforcement system—an agent. With some training we could stamp this out in a hurry!" Mrs. F: "I am for some action, too. How about each parent doing a study with her children? We can get a psychologist to design the questions in a nonthreatening way so we can sit down with the kids and speculate and at least talk about it."

This apparently simple Spectrum Policy has benefits that reach far beyond the problem-solving meeting. We are often asked by managers, "When people come to me with an idea that is clearly impractical, how do I respond without hurting the person and discouraging him from bringing me other, possibly good ideas?" The answer is to use the Spectrum Policy as above. Even an idea that seems clearly impractical to you will have good aspects, since you are never dealing with fools.

Another frequent question is, "How can I correct a subordinate's mistake without stamping out initiative and spirit?" In the case of a mistake, the manager must assume that it was not mischievous or irresponsible, that there was a rationale, and that somehow the incorrect idea or action made sense to the person at the time the mistake was made. An example of this from our laboratory may clarify what we mean. An engine was being developed, and the only remaining bug was how to get dependable carburetion. The mix of fuel and air varied, and sometimes the single-cylinder engine failed to fire. A reasonably good system had been devised. It still produced failures, but the manager hoped that with two weeks' work it could be made reliable, so he promised delivery of the model at the end of that period. The engineer on the project cooperated in making this commitment. Unexpectedly, the manager had to be away from the laboratory for most of the two weeks. The day before delivery the manager (Richard) stopped by to see the engineer (Don). Don and a machinist were feverishly working on an entirely new carburetion system. The new system was approximately as good as the old system. The old, agreed-upon system remained as it had been two weeks before. Richard's promise of delivery was now impossible to meet. Richard saw red but applied the Spectrum Policy.

Richard: Hey, Don, come fill me in on what is happening.
Don: The night you left I was thinking about what should be done with the old system. I was drawing some modifications when I realized again that the real problem

was to draw a predicted amount of vapor into the cylinder. The old system depends on incoming air to pick up enough vapor. Sometimes it does and sometimes it doesn't. It suddenly occurred to me that if we had a huge wicking surface and sprayed on the right amount of fuel, the cylinder would suck it all in every time. Both Jack *(the machinist)* and I were convinced this would correct the problem and be simpler than gimmicking up the old system. I know we are in trouble with delivery. But by the time we got models of the new system working, it was too late to correct the old system, even if it were possible. The new system is not performing perfectly yet. . . .

Richard: Tell me now about your new system.

Don explains it in detail, answering Richard's questions.

Richard: OK, Don, I believe I understand what happened. *Here is what I like about what you did:* You really put your heart into this problem. This new idea is ingenious, and it may give us the final answer—and it sounds patentable. I like the way you thought it through, talked it over with Jack, and committed yourself to make the new system work. *What I am concerned about* is that I am in a hell of a spot on the delivery. We will live through that, but I am trying to think of what you might have done to keep your initiative but also keep me off the spot.

The dialogue that followed was a learning process for Don (and for Richard, too).

The Spectrum Policy in this situation assumes some givens that may not be easy to accept. The first assumption is that the people who work for you are not irresponsible. Second, as a manager, you are more experienced and there is much they can learn from you; therefore part of your responsibility is to teach. Third, people learn faster when they need not defend their personal worth. Fourth, the chewing out method is not only inappropriate between adults, but it is also an inefficient teaching method.

The Spectrum Policy has valuable advantages in any situation. By definition, you first get an understanding of another person's idea or situation because you really lend your mind to it; you temporarily keep quiet about your concerns. This gives you both sides of the problem. Next you talk about what you like in the new idea or situation. This helps to establish that you are discussing an idea or a specific incident and makes clear that your intent is not to put down the man or his idea. Last, you express your concerns.

A teacher was observing her teacher-trainee, who was keeping taut control of the class, tending to turn every point into a lecture, asking rhetorical questions, and discouraging participation by the class.

Teacher: How did it feel to you?

Trainee: I was nervous still, but I believe it went well. I think they really understood the lesson, so I guess it is OK.

Teacher: I like your involvement with your class. It is very evident that you want them to understand, and children do respond to genuine involvement. It appeared to me that you gave them too little chance to join the discussion. When you listen to your tape ask yourself at what points you might have let them do a little talking. I find it more relaxing for me and more fun for them if I deliberately plan to let the kids respond for about half the time.

This procedure is particularly useful for developing a productive interchange between subordinate and boss, for it can work both ways.

Department store supervisor to his assistant: Your salesgirls are spending too much time on coffee breaks when there are customers waiting. I want you to write a memo about it and have each one initial it when she has read it.

Assistant: OK. It is bad business to keep customers waiting and I will do something about it right away. I am concerned whether the memo will make the point as well as a personal discussion would. Is it all right with you if I have a meeting with some of the girls and talk the problem over with them?

The authoritarian supervisor above should be learning to operate differently, and this procedure is an effective way to help him. Not everyone will respond to this approach, but even if he does not, you have reacted constructively and the relationship will be out in the open.

Do not mistake this mode of behavior as mere politeness. It accomplishes results that politeness alone cannot achieve. It not only reflects appreciation for the worth of people—it also permits you to be candid: to give complete information without damage to the person. Since it makes honesty nondestructive, it can lead to a better, more supportive, realistic relationship between boss and subordinate.

HOW MEETING STRUCTURE CHANGES

The basic unit of a meeting is two people. In fact, the same dynamics occur in a meeting between two persons as in one between ten or twenty persons. Having more people causes multiplied reactions and complexities, but the feelings are the same. A good meeting produces learning and change in everyone, and these depend upon involvement. In general, involvement decreases as the size of the meeting increases, and, from our experience, when more than seven people participate in a meeting it becomes difficult to use all the individuals enough to keep them involved. When meetings larger than seven seem necessary, ask yourself what the real purpose is. If problem solving and development of alternatives are primary, try arranging the members in work groups no larger than seven; then in the last ten or fifteen minutes have a spokesman report for each group its possible solutions.

Each person's needs and motives remain the same as the meeting gets larger, but the effects of behaviors seem to magnify. For example, in a two-person meeting if A puts down B's idea, B can instantly react in defense and try to repair the damage to his self-image. The more witnesses to B's put-down, the more serious the damage seems to be. Another factor that tends to magnify effects is the presence of higher authority.

So as the number and importance of people at the meeting increase, every action matters more. At the same time it becomes more difficult to guide the meeting. The leader must rely on structure and enforce behavioral rules much more carefully in a large meeting than in a small.

MEETING ROLES

There are appropriate roles for each participant in a meeting. If these are understood and adhered to, the probability of success can be substantially increased.

In traditional meetings each participant operates at two different levels. At one level he recognizes the organization of the meeting. He assumes that the chairman is in charge and that he himself is there to help solve someone else's problem. There are three recognizable roles here: leader, expert, participant.

In actuality each participant operates at a second level, too. At this level he shifts from one role to another whenever he feels the need. He may take over leadership with an idea, a criticism, or a dissertation. He may become the expert or simply try to be helpful. Because roles are not clearly defined there is confusion, and when we analyze tapes of such meetings we find repeated evidence of behavior that works against the meeting's probability of success. For example, there is a high level of antagonism toward ideas. People identify with their own ideas and this antagonism is perceived as a personal attack. The extent and effects of these attacks are quite remarkable.

To get some measurement of the effect of seemingly mild antagonism, we experimented with a psychogalvanometer—a device that measures and reads out on a dial changes in skin resistance.[3] Electrodes are attached to two fingers of the subject, and the pointer is brought to a normal reading for the subject. In our experiment we then said to him in a quiet voice, "I am not upset or anything, but I am going to gently slap your arm." We gave the subject's arm a gentle slap. In about fifteen seconds the pointer rose sharply. Later, in a meeting with the subject, we waited until he proposed an idea. The act of voicing an idea made the pointer climb, suggesting some emotional investment. When his pointer settled down we used a familiar cliché, "I hate to be negative but," and we found some fault with the subject's idea. He remained outwardly calm and reasonable, but the pointer jumped as though we had slapped him.

Other common occurrences in meetings are:

You often don't get a chance to speak your mind. This is particularly bothersome if you are generally reticent.

If you are not expert in the problem being discussed, your speculations are not valued. (And quite often you do not even contribute them.)

The leader or chairman does most of the talking.

The meeting wanders off the track.

The leader selects those ideas of which he approves and ramrods them through. (He often gives his own ideas special treatment.)

People frequently get flashes of ideas that are out of the context of the conversation at that moment. These may be forgotten and lost, or the person may tune in his idea and drop out of the meeting.

These and other difficulties tend to make a meeting a collection of competing individuals instead of a team. The multiplicative power of teamwork is lost.

---

[3] These experiments are just beginning and can hardly be considered definitive. We really don't know what we are measuring. The important fact is, however, that everyone responds actively to antagonism. A sensitive awareness of your own experience will support this.

The first inkling we got in our research that the structure might be wrong occurred in 1963. There were eight in our group. Since meetings were our business, we held a lot of them. Usually two or three of our company were busy or away, so the average meeting consisted of four or five and the leader. The leader was not formally chosen or elected, but by custom one of my partners, Bill Gordon, or I led. In retrospect, I see that we were the two most aggressive people in the company. I discovered that I was quite critical of the way Bill led the group, believing, "objectively, of course," that I could do a more effective job. Bill and I discussed this, and I was surprised to find that he felt critical about my leadership. A year later, when we were working with client groups, we questioned each member about the leadership. Without exception each person believed that he could do a better job than the acting leader. Some qualified that by this sort of remark: "Of course, I am not used to leading, and I am not really that type, but if I were, I could run a more effective meeting."

We now believe that this kind of dissatisfaction is universal. The best that can be done is to mitigate the condition. One course is to change radically the responsibilities of the leader. Since power is implicit in leadership, the problem becomes one of using that power to engage the capabilities of the individuals in the group and utilizing its collective strength to attack the problem at hand—in such a way that this does not arouse resentment. Our approach was to clarify the difference in tasks between the leader and the members. Another way to reduce team dissatisfaction is to make everyone a leader.

THE ROLE OF THE LEADER

The role of the leader as we describe it here has evolved through ten years of experimentation. After attempts at meetings where *everyone* had equal power without a leader and observations of groups who were left to decide on their own what they wanted to do about leadership (as in the thermos experiment), it became obvious that, for reasons we have already discussed, the chances for a successful meeting were reduced if there was no functioning leader.

In the transcript of the thermos experiment you could probably observe in each participant a strong current of self-service. Psychiatrists know that self-regard is a necessary component of a healthy personality, and one should not seek to lose one's identity in meetings. Quite the contrary. The goal is to make maximum use of each individual personality and style to generate diverse possibilities for creativity. What we want to change is the behavior that is destructive and that interferes with the purpose of the problem-solving meeting.

We find that such behaviors do not surprise our course participants; what surprises them is the *degree* of destructiveness and the existence of such patterns in themselves. It is part of man's instinct for self-preservation that each person thinks of himself as the exception: the one who behaves decently. It comes as a shock to learn the far-reaching consequences of certain common and accepted actions.

We needed a new type of meeting and a new type of chairman or leader: a new situation which would never expect or press group members to defend themselves or their ideas. Relieved of the burden of self-protection, everyone could channel all his energies toward solving the problem. As a result of our experiences with and without traditional chairmen or leaders, we found ourselves moving in two directions. First we gradually changed the responsibilities of the leader to make him more acceptable to the group. Second, we decided that everyone should have the opportunity to taste the responsibilities of leading without rivalry from his teammates.

As we designed the leader's job, we differentiated his responsibilities from those of the other group members.

For if the leader or chairman competes with his group, as he almost always does in traditional meetings, then the competition, the battle for self-preservation, is resumed; group members devote themselves to winning, and the leader tries to control everyone and win himself. It is never a fair contest: the leader nearly always gets his way because he holds the power. His responsibilities form a set of tactics to use with the group. Once specified, they seem obvious, but that does not change the well-documented fact that they are seldom observed. Given the usual emotional dynamics of meetings, it is necessary for the leader to have in mind these particular points. I should add that I am setting forth these points before detailing the Synectics procedure because Synectics cannot work unless the leader is so conscious of this style of leadership that it becomes virtually instinctive to him.

Never Go into Competition with Your Team

People quite often object to this rule at first: "But I have ideas, too. Isn't it more constructive for me to put them in the pot?" This is an important point. We do not want to lose *any* ideas that might be useful. However, we know from experience that if the leader contributes his ideas throughout the meeting he will, unconsciously, favor them. His team is hypersensitive to this, and it reduces its commitment and the probability of success. In Synectics procedures there are specific times when the leader may contribute his ideas. They are welcome during steps called Suggestions (early possible solutions) and Force Fit (pressing for ideas later in the meeting),[4] but he should offer them when there is no other action. If a member voices an idea the leader should support it, usually restating it to make certain he thoroughly understands what the member had in mind. If he can then add to, build on, or strengthen the idea, he should do so. After

---

[4] These steps will be discussed in detail in subsequent chapters.

every member's idea is thoroughly explored, the leader may introduce his own. The general rule, however, is that the leader always gives the idea of every member precedence over his own.

Be a 200 Percent Listener to Your Team Members

The leader's skill in good listening has a pervasive effect on the group's productivity. During a session, the leader carries out repeated transactions with each member. He hears each person and proves that he has understood. He establishes his intent: "My job is to understand what you have in mind and help your thought along. I am not here to make judgments." This posture both gives satisfaction to members and creates an atmosphere where all ideas are assumed to be worthy of consideration by the group.

Do Not Permit Anyone to Be Put on the Defensive

The leader assumes there is value in any notion a member offers. His task is to search out that value, no matter how wild or slack the statement may appear. Humor and laughter are often used as a before-the-fact defense against attack. You can easily retreat to, "I wasn't really serious about this idea." A good leader probes laughter not only for the above reason, but also because the elegance of an emerging idea may be intuitively pleasing before anyone is consciously aware of what the idea really is. The value of such intuitive urgings must not be underestimated.

The leader has a number of procedures for reinforcing an atmosphere of nondefensive response:

1. In his acceptance of metaphorical contributions, he never requires justification. For instance:

Leader: My Question is for an Example. From the world of climatology give me an Example of confusion.
Irving: Road signs on an expressway on a rainy night.
Leader writes: Road signs.
Leader: Tell me more, Irving.
Irving: Well, you are moving fast even though you can't see

really well, and there is a kind of confusion because you are not sure you are responding to the right sign.

Leader: If I get you, you are zipping along at 65 when probably you should be going slower because of the rain—when signs pop into your sight you feel a little mixed up as to whether it is the one you are looking for or not.

Irving: Yes, it is an uncomfortable feeling.

Leader: OK, are there any other Examples of confusion from climatology?

Irving's Example of road signs did not really fit the leader's specification, but the leader bought it anyway and treated it with respect. He then reiterated his question in the hope of steering other members back to climatology. Of course, it is quite possible that Irving's Example may trigger a new line of thought in one of the other members. The point is that the leader suggests directions but never insists on any.

2. If one member disagrees with another's statement during the metaphorical part of the Excursion, the leader accepts both points of view as potentially useful. For instance, suppose the group is examining the concept of filibuster.

Pat: A filibuster goes counter to the intent of the democratic process and should not be permitted.

Jerry: I don't see it that way at all. It permits a determined minority who may be right to bring concentrated attention to its dissent. They may even effect a compromise.

The leader records both thoughts. Thinking of the purpose of the meeting, who is to determine ahead of time which response will prove more valuable?

3. When it is time to press for ideas it is often necessary for the leader to enforce the Spectrum Policy. If he sees that a member (the expert is specially prone to this) is going to respond negatively, he interrupts to ask him, "Tell us what you *like* about what Robert has said."

4. When an idea falters, the leader tries to keep it alive by stressing its generality and asking for help. In the thermos-

closure meeting, Al suggested the use of springs (line 50). The discussion might have gone like this:

Al: Well, of course, you could always use springs.

Paul: Isn't that a hinge?

Leader: Let's not be too concerned with the hinge problem for the moment. Al, what do you have in mind?

Al: I'm not sure, but I thought we could use some sort of a spring that would hold the thing closed.

Leader: You know, this spring idea is intriguing. A spring has, in a sense, two postures—one has energy stored, and in the other the energy is released. Can we use this to help us?

Al: This idea of two different positions—one might be open and the other closed.

Rita: How about this! *(drawing)* The spring has a membrane on one side, and each end of the spring is attached to the side of the mouth here. You have a knob sticking up to work it. In the open position the spring pushes against this side. In the closed, it's against the other side, and the membrane covers the mouth.

Open

Closed

Membrane

Spring Pulled Over

Paul: We could make the membrane out of close-pore sponge and get insulation.

By protecting the beginning idea from Paul and by building and asking for help, the leader thus kept a weak idea alive until it was given strength.

5. If, after every attempt at building has been made, an idea is still lacking in substance, the leader does not finally condemn it.

Leader: OK, it seems we cannot use this idea right now. Let's put it aside, and maybe it will help us later.

This is not idle politeness. We have often seen an idea that has been put aside early in a problem-solving session reappear in a later context and become a key element in a possible solution.

6. The leader avoids pinning down an individual. He does not say, "Harry, give me an example of confusion from the field of climatology." Rather, he addresses such requests to the entire group. No one should be put under pressure to produce an analogy.

KEEP THE ENERGY LEVEL HIGH

This may seem an impossible assignment, but it is not. The energy of the group depends on many things, including some the leader *cannot* control, such as a hangover. But there is much he can do toward keeping interest high. Here are some suggestions that have worked for us. Perhaps you can improvise some others.

1. Your own interest, alertness, and intensity are contagious, so when you take over leadership, give it your best. Don't be reluctant to use body English to underscore your involvement with the group. Moving around, moving close to the member who's talking, gesturing with your hands—anything that's comfortable for you will help to keep the group active.
2. Select elements to discuss that are most interesting to *you*. If *you* are caught up in the proceedings, you will show it, and your team will respond accordingly.
3. Keep the meeting moving at a fast pace. Watch your team members. You can quickly spot the beginnings of boredom, and you must counteract it. Don't spend too long on any one step.
4. Humor is invaluable. If amusing associations occur to you, bring them out. When team members joke, show you enjoy it, too (if you do). You are probably not a professional comedian, so don't try to be. Just be yourself, encourage humor, but do not let the session degenerate into repeated storytelling.

5. Be demanding. Ask difficult questions. Show your appreciation of strangeness, but of course do not find fault with the obvious.

Use Every Member of Your Team

In nearly every group there are quiet members and talkative members. You cannot afford to miss the contributions of the shy ones. Keep mental notes of who makes contributions. Don't pin down a quiet member, but when you have asked for a response, rest your eyes on him first, if he does not respond, then look at the others.

You will, on occasion, have a group member who dominates the session. He will have immediate responses and will go into endless detail. These people are usually bright and valuable, but they can ruin a meeting if permitted to run free. The leader must control such people without alienating them (one may be your boss). Here are three methods we have found useful for dealing with such situations:

1. When you believe you have understood the points he is making, say something like, "Thank you. If I understand your point," and briefly restate it to see if you have comprehended it.
2. Avoid the compulsive talker's eyes when you ask for a response.
3. When you ask for a response, look at someone away from the talker and hold up your hand toward him in a casual stop sign.

If none of these methods is effective, and if it is impractical to have a frank talk with him (using Spectrum!), ask him to listen to a tape recording of the session.

Do Not Manipulate Your Team

The most sensitive instrument for detecting manipulation is people. Manipulation is dishonest and destructive to everyone who is involved. People, because of past experience, are watchful for signs that you are trying to lead them down a path preconceived by you.

If you, as leader, know where you are going, you are not going anywhere. Any false enthusiasm will be apparent and suspect. You do have clear, legitimate authority and responsibility to make certain choices in procedure; these choices aim the members' minds in a specific direction. But beyond that you must not ask leading questions or try to control responses to fit your taste. Similarly, the leader should be careful to avoid choosing his own particular goals at the start of an exploration of ideas. Such a choice will signal to the group that he is serving himself. The leader contributes goals but he does not use his own.

Leading without manipulation is difficult but critical. People ask, "How can I project energy and enthusiasm when I don't feel either. Isn't it faking if I do?" Or they ask, "When the group is not giving me interesting responses, what do I do then?"

Between the stages of first learning the Synectics procedure and finally mastering it often comes a time of some frustration. The newness of the method has worn off, but you have not yet perfected your use of it. This is the time when boredom and disillusionment may be greatest. After continued use of the method and some experiment with wording your responses to the group, you begin to devote your attention more to what is happening and less to the method. The excursions into the unfamiliar will begin to move more naturally both for you and the group members and will become more enjoyable as a result. For instance, as you develop skill in listening you discover that you hear more things that interest you. It is like playing football: at first it is hard work as the team drills and struggles with the mechanics. Later, it becomes more fun as you devote less energy to learning the rules and the plays. Then the team works together harmoniously and effectively with increasing pleasure in the group task of winning football games.

1. Keep notes of what is happening on easel pads in front of your group.
2. When you move from one step to the next, make this clear by the question you ask and by what you write on the pad.
3. When the group is deeply involved in a discussion of a metaphorical point, restate where you are when you want to go on to another response. This helps to keep the excursion moving and helps keep the team with you.

Keep Your Eye on the Expert

When ideas are offered, watch his reactions. Always enforce the Spectrum Policy, but when the expert shows interest in an idea, try to give him more of whatever he wants. If he responds to a line of speculation, urge him to take over. Most of the time the team will produce only tenuous connections. If the expert is working hard, he will be listening for clues—statements that are *suggestive* of a new approach. These may not be valid in themselves, but with his in-depth knowledge he can reshape them and make them valuable.

Keep in Mind That You Are Not Permanent

That is, perhaps, more a rule than a principle. Since groups are less effective with no leader than with one, and since each member, perhaps unconsciously, wants to be a leader, a good compromise is rotation of leadership.

When you know that you will get your chance to lead, you are more willing to commit yourself to another's path of thought even if you are critical of it. This rotation procedure engages strong motives to stay with an idea and cooperate with the leader. You learn conclusively that if you doze and doodle while Sam leads, Sam's mind will be elsewhere when *you* lead. Every leader discovers that he needs all the support he can get. (This in itself is a significant discovery.)

In summary, it is clear that the leadership of a Synectics session requires a superman. It is helpful to realize that being the leader is a full-time job. Doing it well will leave you no time or energy to try to act like a member of the group while leading. No one can possibly hold to all these principles at one time. Keep in mind that you, too, will make mistakes. But if you learn to observe most of the rules, most of the time you will demonstrate to your group that your intentions are good. Members will overlook an occasional slip, particularly when they have experienced the demands of leadership.

THE ROLE OF THE EXPERT

The role of the expert is as important as the role of the leader. As the member with the most complete factual understanding of the problem, he is the one in the position to determine best the relative merits and faults of possible solutions. As a result of his superior knowledge, he is called upon in a Synectics session to attempt the difficult job of fence-straddling as group participant and expert. This dual role demands extra effort, particularly when ideas are being evaluated.

Early in the meeting the expert gives enough background and understanding of the problem so the group can begin to work. No attempt should be made, however, to make the other members of the group as knowledgeable as he is. He will be present to keep everyone honest. The leader determines when the group knows enough to proceed.

As the expert explains the problem, immediate Suggestions often occur to members. The expert observes Spectrum Policy when evaluating these. This added information sparks more immediate ideas, and so on. If the expert is skillful, he can frequently convert these ideas into useful possible solutions by reacting constructively. Unfortunately, there is real pressure on the expert to be defensive. In the traditional view (and he may believe this), the problem is his and he ought to be able to solve it. Also, he may believe that he should have considered everything that these amateurs might think of. So an expert's typical reaction to a familiar idea might be, "Yeah, well, thanks, but I have thought of that and here's what's wrong with your idea." Or he might easily focus on a familiar element of the proposed solution and use that element to pigeon-hole the whole idea with the comment, "We tried that in 1960 and it didn't work because. . . ." These reactions hurt group effectiveness and reduce the probability that the expert will get much help from his team. We find that here again the Spectrum Policy is especially valuable: by focusing first on the part of an idea that seems helpful and *then* pointing out weaknesses, the expert will encourage the group to build on each idea as much as it can. The overriding purpose is not to sugar-coat or be polite; it is to give *complete* information.

> *Problem:* Devise an ice tray that will conveniently, quickly, and easily release ice. It must be superior to anything already on the market.
>
> Barney: How about a coat of Teflon over the tray and the separator?
>
> Expert: Do you mean a layer that is bonded to the surfaces that are in contact with the ice?
>
> Barney: Yes, I do.
>
> Expert: What I like about what you are saying is that you are putting a kind of ice-repellent material between the ice and the tray. It could be very thin, one molecule thick, perhaps, so the cost of material would not matter. My concern is what material we might use. We tried Teflon, and ice sticks to it. Ice, freezing in place, is very strange stuff. While it is liquid, it seems to seek places to hang on to. When it freezes, it really has a grip.

Thus, this expert does at least six important things for the group:

1. He proves that he is there to find ideas that will work. ("What I like . . .")

2. He shows that he is not going to build his ego at the expense of group members' suggestions—Barney is not put down for suggesting a discarded idea (Teflon).

3. He indicates the sort of direction that will be acceptable. (When other directions arise, he will recognize them, also.)

4. He proves that he will listen. ("Do you mean . . . ?")

5. He builds on what was suggested. (". . . repellent . . ." thin, one molecule thick . . . cost would not matter . . .")

6. He helps the team understand more about the problem. ("Ice freezing . . . strange stuff . . .")

As the members listen to what the expert is wishing for ("What I like . . . repellent . . . one molecule thick"), each of them searches his own experiences and feelings to see if he can supply an idea that will satisfy the requirements and become a useful possible solution.

After the expert and the group have dealt with all of the immediate suggestions, the leader makes the decision to move to the next step. He wants the team wrung out of ideas but not bored. When in doubt he moves ahead to the formal development of Goals as Understood. Everyone, including expert and leader, writes as many of these imagined or wished-for or dream solutions from as many points of view as he is able.

When the leader selects a Goal for the Excursion, he should test it with the expert. At this point the expert must tolerate loose and impossible thinking. This is not the time for rigor; that will come later. However, if the wish expressed or implied in the goal were to be fulfilled, and it would still not help the expert when he goes back to deal with the problem, it is quite proper for him to explain this to the leader. Perhaps one of them has misunderstood the goal, or, more likely, a better goal could be selected. There is another occasion on which communication between leader and expert is important. When a Viewpoint or possible solution is finally hammered out, the leader should ask the expert to put it in his own words. The expert should be careful to include enough in his statement of the Viewpoint so that the whole idea can be reconstructed for nongroup associates several weeks later.

It is best for the expert to maintain the attitude that the group is working for him, to help him solve *his* problem. By seeing his relationship to the group in this way, the expert is aware that it is in his interest to keep the group's energy level high by trying to turn its ideas into possible solutions. This also should help him to remember that the group is probably incapable of presenting him with miraculous, completed solutions to his problem; rather, they will provide possible *clues*. It is up to the expert to take these clues and, using his more complete knowledge, turn them into solutions. If you will refer to the Excursion on the oil-well-coring problem in the Personal Analogy section (page 154), you will see how one expert created a new line of speculation from such a clue.

> Kent: You stroke it just like a cat and it calms down.
> Bob *(the expert, musingly)*: Yeah . . . you got to stroke it . . . stroke that oil . . . *(and a few seconds later)* chill it . . . cool it down.

In the early stages of these clues, the expert must listen extra hard to the group members. Often they don't really know what they're saying, in the sense of a completed solution. They usually are playing with a particular point of speculation, trying to express the beginnings of an association or idea in some coherent form. The expert must try, so as not to miss the *germ* of an idea which might help solve his problem, to avoid tempting pitfalls. He must not second-guess a member's thought by assuming he understands a new idea before it has been fully verbalized: he may miss a chance for a new insight. Similarly, he must not label or categorize ideas by assuming that they are merely new examples of old, discarded approaches. Too often, labeling is unjustified, and an idea is prematurely put in the wrong mental category; the danger is that restrictions will be applied that are old prejudices and not really appropriate.

Another technique that is helpful to the expert is to constructively distort the group's ideas. This is not an attempt to deceive the group—it is all done openly and consciously. The expert interprets a clue in a way that might make it helpful even though it has not been verbalized that way. An example will help clarify this point. In the ice-tray problem the group has examined freedom. At Force Fit (pressing for ideas) Tom has a thought that seems, if taken literally, too far-fetched to be useful.

> Tom: Freedom says to me, Let's not have any ice tray at all. Let's make the ice cubes out in the open.
> Leader: You're saying if we can form the ice in the open it can't get a grip and stick to anything?
> Tom: Yeah, if we could just . . .
> Expert: You know, if we forget the cube shape, Tom, what you are suggesting is something like an icicle. We might have a series of little leaks in the tray and grow icicles. . . .

In reality, Tom was not suggesting icicles. The expert constructively misunderstood.

The expert encourages the group when he defers judgment of an idea until the group builds it as strong as it can. This does *not* mean, however, that the expert sits back and lets the group fumble around without his help. Rather he intervenes to give support to the ideas to explain what he likes. Here is where the expert's role is most difficult: he must jump back and forth between supporting an idea on the one hand, and voicing realistic concerns on the other. He is never to be a pushover, to let a weak idea pass as a strong possible solution. The group can tell he's letting them off easily. But he must be careful when he points out weaknesses to be sure that it doesn't come across to the group as an attack or rejection. It is always best to point out the strengths of an idea *first* (the Spectrum Policy); then to ask how we can get around the problem of such-and-such.

Below is a different example of constructive behavior on the part of an expert. In one of our training sessions, a group of engineers was trying to develop a new type of fuel cell. The expert had spent two years working on the problem. After their first excursion, about thirty minutes long, the group arrived at a possible solution. When the expert had finally evaluated it, his comment to them was: "This is amazing! Do you know, you guys have developed a concept in half an hour that it took four years to develop back in 1918!" The other members of the group naturally felt quite good, and in their next excursion they developed another concept in about forty-five minutes. His next evaluation kept them feeling good: "It took me eighteen months of steady work before I came up with that last year. And now you've done it in forty-five minutes!" Even though it was 5:30, the end of a long day of training, the group felt energetic enough to try another excursion. After a thirty-minute session, they produced a possible solution which was new to the expert, and which suggested an entirely new type of fuel cell. In this example, the expert got across the same factual information about the first two possible solutions as if he had said, "For heaven's sake, they invented that type of fuel cell back in 1918! I thought you were supposed to come up with something new!" But with critically better results.

These two types of responses cover the range from extremely constructive to extremely destructive, and their effects on the group are clear.

Another technique that is valuable for experts is to back off from the specifics of an idea that seems unworkable and turn it into a generality. Again, the expert must listen hard for the clue to a new approach, trying to get the *idea behind a suggestion* without getting caught in unnecessary details. The specific suggestion might involve the use of Teflon; while the expert may know that Teflon itself is not a realistic choice, the *idea* of such a material could be. The expert can pick up this basic concept and look for alternative methods—for example, use silicones instead of Teflon. Thus the generality of a material slippery to water and ice is not thrown out with an unacceptable specific. Frequently, the leader can help preserve an idea in the same way. He need not have an alternative in mind; to translate an idea to its generality can be enough to keep it alive.

The expert has a profound effect on the group's energies. His response to ideas at Force Fit time can determine whether or not a session is successful. It is in his interest to provide the group with as much *honest* support as possible. (Faked support and false enthusiasm are easily detected.) Another procedure that seems to encourage the group is note-taking by the expert. This is especially true when the Force Fit provides Viewpoints that are outside the expert's domain. By writing down Viewpoints and telling of his intention to investigate them, the expert demonstrates his evaluation of their efforts.

A final suggestion for the expert: it is helpful if he can be temporarily irresponsible and dismiss all of the real-world restrictions during the developing stages of an idea. The more freely the expert speculates, the easier it is for the group to do likewise.

THE ROLE OF THE PARTICIPANT

Participants are the heart of any meeting. All the skills of the leader and the constructive responses of the expert are designed to help each participant make his unique contributions. To emphasize the true relationships in a meeting we view the leader as a servant to the group. The group is, of course, servant to the problem. The expert is the problem's representative, and except in matters of behavior his opinions are honored. Differences with him are welcomed too, as you will see. An important point that is often lost is that a meeting is held to make use of the mind of each participant. The leader and expert can be successful only when they engage the participants. But a good participant will discipline himself also. Knowing the steps in the process and the kind of behavior that promotes success, he will bend his impulses toward cooperation.

As the meeting opens, the immediate objective is understanding of the problem at hand. The leader writes up a brief general statement of the problem (Problem as Given), and the expert describes the problem.

> Leader writes: How to get a boss to make decisions?
> Expert: My boss is a terrific procrastinator, and it is driving us crazy.

The expert gives the whole team a new understanding of the problem. Each member, in a slightly different way, will convert the problem to personal terms; for example, "I have a boss. He has put off decisions. I know what that feels like. What did I do then? I did something that worked or thought of some action that might work." At this point this member is ready to try out a suggestion on the expert.

> Member A: Something I have tried with some success is to ask for a decision by a certain date.
> Expert: I like the idea of scheduling an end point. That puts some pressure on him to get to it. It also gives me an excuse to come and bug him about it. I've tried this with him, and while he approved of scheduling he simply ignores it.
> Leader: Can we give the scheduling idea more influence somehow?
> Member B: Scheduling made me think of what *after* a decision. What if you attached to important proposals a set of completion dates—you know, estimates of the time required.
> Leader: Interesting! You show the consequences of delay. *(To expert)*: What do you think?
> Expert: That is interesting. I'd never thought of it . . . mak-

ing it explicit, I mean. I have assumed he knew. I like that. It is simple and realistic.

The difference here is that the leader assumes A's suggestion, though not new, has implications that may be valuable. So does the expert. So does Member B. He listened, let the schedule idea trigger his thought, and built a new dimension into the idea. Every attempt at building will not result in a successful idea; however, it nearly always increases understanding, it prevents ideas from being discarded, and it signals the other members what manner of man (or woman) you are.

As participant your most valuable contributions will come from using your sensitivity to trigger speculation in yourself and presenting the group with the fruit of that speculation if it seems in any way helpful. If the team is stumped you can often get it moving by offering raw speculation without knowing whether it will help.

> Member C: *(to expert)* When you said "excuse" I began to think of when I was a kid going to school. I would spend most of the walk to school thinking of excuses for my arithmetic teacher.
> Member D: Taking that excuse idea is there some way we could give the boss an excuse in case his decision is wrong? Probably he hates decisions because they may be wrong.

Your underlying intent will be reflected in your behavior. When you intend to help solve the problem you will employ your sensitivity and aggression toward that end. You must resist the pull of old habits that urge you to spot weaknesses in ideas and expose them. You will be far more useful and will get more satisfaction if you spot a weakness and think of a cure for it.

In a real sense each individual is a one-man team. Consider the many roles you play every day: father or mother, teacher, businessman, learner, buyer, organizer, friend, and so on. Consider that you have been observing and collecting experiences in problem solving from birth. Any one or combination of these experiences may give you a personal feeling for a problem, the desire for possible solution, the associations to start speculation, and a reality to test against.

This remarkable memory bank is so taken for granted and devalued that most of us ignore it in most situations as irrelevant. This is worse than waste; it is crippling not to exercise this complex but beautifully integrated capability. Without daily use, this capacity works restlessly on dreams and we forget what we are able to do.

The major charge to each participant is to make use of his total self.

4
A Theory of Creative Thought

Good behavior is a powerful tool for group accomplishment but only part of the answer to the problem of group creativity. Problems that have been worked and reworked require fresh approaches; otherwise, people keep seeing the same problem in much the same way and get caught in the same restrictions. Then it is not enough just to encourage oneself and fellow group members to behave constructively.

When we repeatedly observed that almost no one used the step-by-step procedures they developed for solving the thermos problem, we concluded that such procedural outlines might be reasonably accurate descriptions of remembered actions but were of little value in engaging the individuals' creative capabilities. The fact that these procedures were so uniformly abandoned led us to believe that people must naturally work and think some other way. Our task was to identify this other way of thinking. We could then try to discover which elements of the other way of thinking were most constructive—that is, which increased understanding and speculation—and which elements were most destructive—tended to reduce or stop speculation.

Our methods in this phase of the research may be interesting to you. From 1963 to the present we have used the thermos problem. As mentioned earlier, we varied group make-up from people who met a few minutes before the experiment (as in the transcript) to a group leader and group who had worked together for years; some groups included the president, a vice president, and men several rungs down the ladder from them. We varied the amount of time allowed from thirty minutes to a few hours. We tried various environments—company conference room, sylvan retreat, our workrooms; we have even had several groups do the experiment in front of an audience. The variety of people in the groups has been enormous: scientists, students, ministers, businessmen, Peace Corps volunteers and returnees, and a fair representation of nationalities—American, British, French, German, Nigerian, Ghanaian, Indian. Each group was tape-recorded and the tape examined. In nearly all cases the same modes of response were there. In spite of a high level of destructive response, many groups arrived at good solutions. Because we know the sort of start that *can* lead to a good solution, we have learned to identify the kind of behavior that (a) produces such a start and (b) cuts it off before it can gain strength.

Once this identification was made, we could try to combine the constructive ways of thinking with the constructive ways of behaving and incorporate both into a procedure for problem-solving meetings. In fact, we actually had identified many of these ways of thinking before we became aware of the vast importance of other behavioral elements.

The most constructive element in the other way of thinking is the use of metaphor.[1] Although it is not always done consciously, group members and people in general make analogies between their problem and another object or idea. You will recall the balloon, the colander, and the iris closure from the thermos problem. When these analogies are explored by the groups, they often bring a wealth of new material to the problem—contexts and ways of

---

[1] "A figure of speech in which a word or phrase literally denoting one kind of object or idea is used in place of another by way of suggesting likeness or analogy between them" (*Webster's Seventh New Collegiate Dictionary*). For example, "a mighty fortress is our God," or, "the ghetto was a volcano about to erupt."

speculating that never come up if the members concentrate only on the specifics of the problem.

Let us consider the colander closure from the transcript. In that case it was not explored, but using the material from another group, let's look at what might have been done:

Paul: Also, the colanders, you know, the kitchen colanders that come together. Well, it's the same idea as the cups that you use at camp that fold up; maybe you could have something that could turn and would come out as you turned it.

Harry: That telescoping idea could be great. It could disappear into the neck. . . . Could we keep it from leaking?

Al: Yes. Have just one link, or whatever you call it, in the telescope. You pull it out and there is a hole in the side.

Rita: And the hole is big enough to get a spoon in. You turn the bottle on its side and you can eat your stew.

John: You put a top on it?

Paul: Yes . . . an insulated top. Make the whole thing of plastic with a tight flange.

There is a high correlation between the use and pursuit of such analogies or examples and the generating of fruitful speculation. We found that this is a repeatable procedure that increases the probability of success. We wanted to know *why* it worked, so first we re-examined the traditional step-by-step procedures which were made up by our many experimental groups and which then were so often abandoned in the heat of battle. We were sympathetic with this abandonment because we ourselves had made up step-by-steps and then ignored them.

Nearly all such procedures have one or two steps that exhort the team to get ideas: "Develop alternatives, give ideas, hypothesize, speculate!" The group in the transcript has three steps that seem to lead toward ideas:

1. Mull the facts over.
2. Speculate.
3. Develop ideas.

"Speculate" captures the essentials of numbers 1 and 3, and over a period of time we tried to discover what it is to speculate and wondered how we could make it more useful than an exhortation. *Webster's* tells us that to speculate is to ponder or theorize about a problem or subject in its various aspects and relationships. If one is to speculate, he must have aspects or relationships as the raw material. Our observations suggest there are three sources for such material.

1. Already known facts about the problem and analysis of these facts.
2. Discovery of new facts that have a bearing on the problem.
3. Your responses to the problem.

Source number 1 is, of course, crucial. If you are to deal successfully with a problem, you must, at some point, become knowledgeable about it. Yet there are two difficulties with source number 1. First, everyone who is concerned with the problem has much the same material to work with. If you carry out a line of speculation, arrive at a viewpoint, reduce it to practice, and put it on the market, chances are that your competitor will not be far behind. Second, a rich background of knowledge in a problem area actually tends to inhibit speculation.

We believe that as the expert accumulates the specific knowledge that makes him so valuable he also incorporates accepted certainties that are not really certain. This explains why, historically, so many innovative breakthroughs have come from outsiders rather than from those who are thought to be most expert in the particular field. Naturally, the most powerful combination is the expert who is willing to suspend temporarily his belief in his certainties and who is willing to speculate in any direction and have comfortable, even cherished, certainties re-examined and questioned by group members who are not even knowledgeable in the area. Men like this are rare. A disproportionate share of the discoveries down the years has been produced by such men—Archimedes, Copernicus, Galileo, Bacon, Newton, Pasteur, Freud, Einstein. The systematic development of this willingness to think the unthinkable, however, is critical if you are to make better use of your potential. You simply never know what errant, seemingly irrelevant thought or observation will clue you toward a solution. When you are solving problems you must keep every sense wide open.

The second source of materials for speculation—new facts—is quite understandable. For example, suppose you are working on the problem of speeding the healing time of wounds. In library research brief mention is made of German concentration camp inmates who used the skin of a fallen aircraft to cover wounds. They obtained remarkably good healing results. This new fact suggests several new paths for speculation; perhaps the rigid airtight covering has an effect; or one of the metals in the aircraft skin; or all of the metals in combination, etc. One of the important reasons for knowledge-extending research is to furnish new facts that may lead to fresh and useful speculation.

A fascinating aspect of new facts is the very wide difference in ability to recognize them as useful. Harold Bogart, a research engineer for Ford, tells of working on the problem of finding a new binder coating for sand grains that would permit faster molding. A number of his engineers studied the patent literature on coatings (a good source of new facts) and found nothing useful. He went through the same material, consciously making the effort to stay loose and not to insist on an exact or even close fit to his problem; in short, he tried to view the patents as metaphorical or suggestive. As a result of his flexibility, he quickly noted a process for coating corks that suggested a promising solution to his problem.

The third source of raw materials for speculation—your response to the problem—cannot accurately be separated from the first two sources. In spite of all attempts to approach problems and their data objectively, people *do* have subjective responses, which are not to be ignored. Even what a person sees and accepts is greatly influenced by his individual personality. As Koestler points out in *The Act of Creation,* a machine-gun officer looking at a ridge will notice good gun emplacements; a timber scout will notice the trees ready for harvest.

Unfortunately, in industry, education and science, we are taught to suppress or conceal our personal responses instead of using them openly for all they are worth. To understand how we can systematically make greater use of our potential, it is helpful to have a view of how the mind works. This view is theoretical and oversimplified.

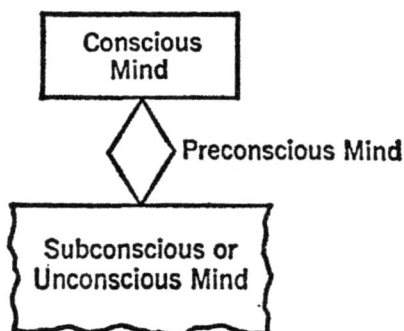

As presented in the diagram above, the conscious mind contains all that one knows that is readily available. This information is well organized and interconnected on a logical basis. The conscious mind is a square shooter. It is characterized by its desire to organize, to make rules of thumb and live by them. For example, if in baseball you hit a long ball that goes foul, the conscious mind would not think of claiming the right to run to first base. Similarly, as Koestler says, in chess, the conscious would not consider moving a knight in a direction not permitted by the rules.

These characteristics of the conscious mind are invaluable for learning, putting in order, and testing hypotheses in a logical way. On the other hand, the conscious mind tends to be inhibited by the very qualities that make it so powerfully useful. It is a skillful pigeonholer. If it can categorize one element of an idea, it stuffs the whole idea into that pigeonhole, ignoring meaningful differences. It lives by the rules and by logic; it resists irresponsible speculation. From our observation, people who rely heavily on their analytic ability find it very difficult to entertain ideas that are foreign to the rules they have learned.

The preconscious[2] is like a problem-oriented, opinionated, independent file clerk. It looks over the shoulder of the conscious mind. When a problem that interests the preconscious is being considered, it conducts a search into the unconscious for clues that it considers relevant.

The unconscious, or subconscious, is a storehouse of immense capacity. According to Freud, it contains everything one has experienced since conception. Jung believed that it contains memories that go back to one's forefathers. Perhaps the most persuasive evidence of the contents of the unconscious comes to us from hypnotists and neurosurgeons. "A small group of subjects was regressed . . . and their memories tested for recall of schoolmates and teachers whose names were inaccessible to them in the waking state . . . they were successful in checking the accuracy of recall by going back to old school records."[3] Another experiment that is suggestive of the completeness of the unconscious record is this: A subject is taken into a crowded cocktail party for one minute. He is then asked to describe the party fully. He gives a few reasonably accurate, general statements about it. When hypnotized, he can tell with much more precision how many people were in the room, the color of the curtains, the type of carpet, and many other details that would go unnoticed by most of the other guests.

---

[2] This theory differs from that of Freud as does my use of "preconscious."

[3] Ernest R. Hilgard, *The Experience of Hypnosis*, p. 172.

As for neurosurgeons, *Time* reported that Dr. Wilder
Penfield of McGill Medical School was operating on a
woman's brain, using local anesthetic. He prodded some
brain cells. The woman exclaimed that he had just caused
her to re-experience a long-forgotten episode in her life
complete with all the sensations, including color. Another
prod produced a different episode, also complete. The
doctor theorized that the brain has a continuous recording
device that stores all that happens to a person. Doctors
using electroencephalographs suggest that this recording
is analogous to moving-picture frames and is done at the
rate of one frame every 0.1 second or ten frames per second, this being based upon the interval between brain
waves. In sum, there is strong evidence that the unconscious mind is a reservoir of information so vast and rich
that it seems quite incredible to the conscious mind.

During the problem-solving process, the preconscious,
when evoked by interest and emotional commitment, goes
searching for relevant suggestive data. Its criteria for relevance do not seem logical because often the data that are
presented do not appear to the conscious mind to be
connected even distantly with the problem at hand. For
this and other reasons people gradually build in a censor
to protect the conscious mind from the overt interrupting
thoughts from the unconscious by way of the preconscious. (The figure below is a representation.)

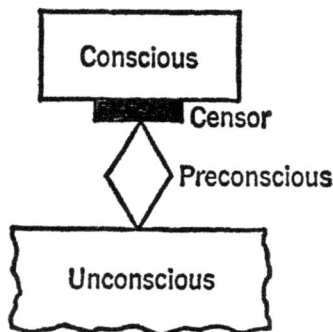

You will note that this censor is below conscious control. Consequently, one cannot open his mind simply by resolving not to block the signals from his unconscious.

There are three observations we can make about this censor. First, it is not infallible. Given desire on the part of a person to solve a problem, and given time and pressure, chances are good that some helpful message will get through. However, a man who is committed and under pressure to solve a difficult problem is a man in some agony. The majority of people prefer not to spend much time in this state. They tackle less difficult problems and reserve such commitment for the hours between nine and five. We believe that in spite of this, nearly everyone is continually solving problems and exhibiting creative capability. One person may spend most of his creative energy on raising his family, another on developing a hypothesis to explain magnetism. We believe that for each person the creative process is the same, and each must fool his censor to get some of his raw material for speculation.

Each of us has come to depend upon one technique or another for getting new ideas. Usually we have arrived at a procedure almost unconsciously by trial and error. A key element in such procedures is the mulling over, sometimes called incubation. This point may come early or after much work, when one seems to have gone as far as he can and is still without a new viewpoint. He temporarily puts the problem out of his mind and takes a vacation from it. This is a matter of degree; some people seem to completely forget the problem, while others temporarily turn their attention to something else. People take this vacation from the problem with some assurance that a clue will come to them. It usually does while shaving, bathing, cutting the grass, driving a familiar route to work, waking from sleep, or going to sleep: each person seems to have a favorite time or activity. In each case the censor is lulled to inattention, and the valuable raw material is slipped past it.

In addition to the famous examples from history (Archimedes and Eureka!, Poincaré descending from the bus, etc.), many people have told us of such experiences. A minister told of his long-time worry over boring his congregation. As he was shaving one morning the thought popped into his consciousness: "Hire theater critics." He felt excited about this thought but did not immediately understand either the thought's significance or his excitement. Puzzling, he suddenly realized this was a way of improving his sermons. He appointed representative observers to give him their reactions after each sermon. His reviews started out poor, but pace and sharpness improved and his congregation increased.

A second observation about the censor is that it appears to have a direct connection with the use of creative potential. If a person has developed sensitivity to the proddings of the unconscious, if his censor is easily bypassed or penetrated, he is able to behave more creatively and use more of his potential. One characteristic of the great discoverers is that they have been very responsive to their own impulses or intuitions. Pasteur repeatedly demonstrated this sensitivity.[4] We believe intuition is an early recognition, *below the conscious level,* that one is on the right track. When this happens, the unconscious tries to give a signal to offer encouragement. A rather simpleminded example of this happens to me. While driving along a rarely traveled throughway I sometimes sense that I am nearing my destination. The scenery is monotonously unfamiliar, there appear to be no significant landmarks but I feel a faint excitement or relief, and in a minute or two, a sign appears. Most of us ignore these signals. Highly productive, creative people have learned, instead, to honor them. As one would expect, intuition

---

[4] W. I. B. Beveridge, *The Art of Scientific Investigation,* pp. 128, 129.

(as does reason) often leads us astray, but for the great discoverer many false leads are far outweighed by the few correct leads that bring breakthroughs.

A third observation about the censor has to do with its formation. Some years ago, just after World War II, psychologists at a university were discussing creativity and age. They agreed that by age forty-five one is over the hill, and creativity is pretty much gone. They decided it would be useful to establish this fact experimentally. They selected test instruments and tested a universe—a cross section—of forty-five-year-olds. To no one's surprise only 2 percent of those tested were highly creative. Discussing the results, one psychologist suggested it would be interesting to find the age when creativity seemed to wear out. The others agreed, and they tested universes of forty-four-year-olds, forty-three-year-olds, and so on. This proved to be a monotonous task because the 2 percent highly creative remained the same until the weary psychologists reached the universe of seven-year-olds, at which point the highly creative jumped to 10 percent. At five years old the figure was 90 percent creative![5]

This suggests that nearly all of us begin life highly creative, but soon after the start of our formal education, the censor begins to build up and creative potential becomes harder to reach. By age eight or nine, logical, analytical thinking has taken over. We gradually slip into the restrictive domain of traditional thought. It is in this sense that our highly analytical training restricts our creativity: we become too logical. Our rich emotional and imaginative resources are largely neglected during education and devalued in most situations after graduation.

Referring again to the transcript, the group's difficulty in arriving at good solutions was due partly to their inability to make use of their creative potential and partly to their destructive, nonsupportive reactions and behavior.

[5] V. J. Papenek, "Solving Problems Creatively," pp. 169–96.

To be able to use their creative potential—to tap the resources of the preconscious, and, through it, the unconscious—people must modify the strangling effect of their education and make better use of life experiences.

This has obvious implications for traditional education and business. We believe these are not so much bad as they are incomplete. An important part of us is ignored both in training and on the job. Because our emotional and imaginative elements are as much a part of us as our intellect or our bodies, this neglect produces a discomfort and uneasiness. We believe that business pays a high penalty for a structure and tradition that leaves such a vital component of its people unused.

It is unrealistic to ask you to change your habits by appealing solely to your logic—though this has its usefulness. Before you make the effort to change, you must experience and observe the results of using these unaccustomed procedures. You must be convinced by evidence you feel and observe that it is in your best interest to entertain and encourage your intuitions, your desires, and your daydreams. It is possible only with great effort and usually only if your conscious mind is convinced that it will be called back into service at the proper moment— that you will not go out of control. For the moment it is the raw material of our imaginations and our feelings that we are interested in. This raw material, the substance of fresh speculation, is the material we observed being brought in by metaphor. It is the function of the preconscious to provide this material for consideration by the conscious.

Perhaps Lawrence Kubie's summary will help to bring this all into focus:

Whence then comes our creative function? To answer this we have to stop for a moment to indicate what we mean by creativity. Clearly, by the creative process we mean the capacity to find new and unexpected connections, to voyage freely over the seas, to happen on America as we seek new routes to India, to find new relationships in time and space, and thus new meanings. Or to put it in another way, it means working freely with conscious and preconscious metaphor, with slang, puns, overlapping meanings, and figures of speech, with vague similarities, with the reminiscent recollections evoked by some minute ingredients of experience, establishing links to something else which in other respects may be quite different. It is free in the sense that it is not anchored either to the pedestrian realities of our conscious symbolic processes, or to the rigid symbolic relationships of the unconscious areas of personality. This is precisely why the free play of preconscious symbolic processes is vital for all creative productivity.[6]

Our research told us that if we use our capacity to make and pursue metaphors, we increase the probability of fresh, unthought-of lines of speculation. The problem then was, How could we make the use of metaphor operational? How could we generate and use this raw material of potential solutions in a controlled and repeatable way? How could we do *consciously* what the great inventors and discoverers seemed to do *un*consciously?

The Synectics system has been called by some an artificial vacation because it seems to let us take a holiday from the problem by not having to think about it consciously for a while, and it encourages us to put aside our business-suit thinking, our usual tight, analytical frame of mind; but it is an *artificial* vacation, because while our conscious enjoys making the analogies our preconscious is hard at work on the problem.

[6] Lawrence S. Kubie, *Neurotic Distortion of the Creative Process*, p. 141.

5
Using Analogies

In any meeting, a leader needs some form of structure for himself and the group to work with. While Synectics encourages flexibility and departure from usual patterns of thought, the process does contain a series of steps to serve as guides, as the leader and the group desire. Our objective is to increase the probability of success in problem solving; the procedure is meant to reinforce constructive behavior and to stimulate preconscious activity. To serve these purposes, the steps may be reordered, improvised upon, or replaced by others. The sequence is not necessarily rigid.

Synectics procedures represent, we believe, the problem-solving process that each of us uses every day. Steps are artificially separated and exaggerated but are faithful to life. This natural process is a complex skill, but everyone develops it to a high degree early in life by solving the enormous problems of walking, talking, using our hands, etc. Because humans learn also to be economical of effort that seems unrewarding (often considered laziness), this skill tends to diminish in school.

The mechanisms presented below, as though for group use only, can be profitably used by individuals alone. One New York executive runs a paper-and-pencil Synectics session every morning during his hour-long commute. Problem solving, like some other skills, can be improved with practice. Hundreds of individuals who have consciously used the mechanisms of Synectics report that they are mentally more limber in dealing with problems. Ideas come more easily, they see possibilities where they before did not—in short, like an athlete in shape, they feel more confident of their capability.

The Problem as Given (abbreviated PAG) is the starting point, a statement of the problem to be attacked. The problem may be handed to you by an outside source or posed by yourself. It is sometimes helpful to substitute the word "opportunity" for "problem."

Analysis is an explanation by the expert of the Problem as Given. As the person most familiar with the problem, the expert is in the best position to know whether the group's final suggestions are helpful. There may be more than one expert at the beginning stage, but later a single expert is designated for each excursion. This may be an artificial designation, like leadership, but it is useful so that possible solutions can be focused toward a single expert. Analysis explanation should be in enough detail so the group has a common understanding of the problem; however, since the expert will be a participant, he need not try to make everyone else as knowledgeable as he is.

Suggestions. As we observed in the thermos session, people tend to jump to immediately apparent solutions to problems, rather than seeking less obvious but potentially better approaches. If unexpressed, these immediate Suggestions may tend to inhibit the participants' ability to think of anything else. It helps, therefore, to encourage people to air their immediate solutions and to discuss them fully. Even if these ideas are not destined for adoption, the experts' explanations of their virtues and flaws will help the group to understand the problem.

Goals as Understood (abbreviated GAU) is a formalization of a step in the natural problem-solving process. When you are understanding a problem you relate it to things or experiences you know. You next imagine solutions that seem to fulfill the demands of the problem. Often your first imagined solutions will be Suggestions.

As you become more skilled you will be able to imagine better, more wishful solutions; these make more useful

Goals as Understood even though they seem less possible to reach. Each participant, including leader and expert, should devise at least one, preferably several, Goals as Understood. The leader then writes them up for all to see. This procedure of formally obtaining each member's personal way of understanding the problem and his dream solutions or goals serves several vital purposes.

First, it permits each member to make the problem his own. We found in our research that each person has his own ways of seeing problems. He apparently cannot agree with another's specific statement without serious reservation. There is no reason why he should. He is there because you want to use his mind. His personal statement of the goal or problem will certainly be useful to him and it may be evocative to the whole group. In our culture there is in chairmen an urge to get consensus about the problem. Endless time is wasted debating a statement of the problem to be worked on. We believe consensus at this point is not only impossible (it seems to violate some basic law of individuality) but undesirable. If the members understand there *are* different views of the problem and that these differences are useful and will be recorded, each can relax about his own slightly different view and stop trying to make converts.

Also, generating Goals as Understood takes advantage of the diversity of individuals in the group, spurring each to see the problem or goal in a way that has not occurred to him before. Wishful thinking at this stage is rewarding, for realistic conservatism restricts speculation. Feel free to wish for *anything* you can imagine, even if it violates laws you *know* hold true. Real-world restrictions will be considered before a final Viewpoint is accepted, but limiting yourself too soon will reduce the probability of innovation.

An example may clarify this point. We were working with a group of architectural students. Their final assignment before graduation was to design a new building for the school of architecture at their own university. We were discussing this problem and working toward Goals.

> Student: One thing I would like is a locker or locked space in the studio area where I could keep my things.
> Leader: Would you like a private studio of your own?
> Student: Oh, no! We could not afford that.
> Leader: Suppose you could afford it?
> Student: Well, anyway, that would not be fair, you know, to the others.
> Leader: OK, everyone has a private studio. Would you like that?
> Student (*doubtfully*): I guess so.
> Leader: You know, that is a wish, a dream solution. But we don't want to wish for something you would not want if we got it.
> Class: We would each like a private studio.

This was written up as one of many goals. A day or so later one leader selected it as a goal to work on, and the group developed a possible solution that would fill their specifications, give each student a private studio, and cost less than a traditional approach. They combined dormitory rooms with studio space.

It is possible they decided finally not to use this solution, but the alternative was there for consideration. The chances are very small that they would have arrived at this Viewpoint if they had not been willing to make that seemingly impossible wish.

Also, generating Goals as Understood helps to break complex problems into manageable parts. This is particularly helpful with problems concerning people, which always have many different aspects.

Finally, when the leader selects a Goal as Understood the group's attention is focused on that specific aspect of the problem. Since each member knows which approach is being used, teamwork is reinforced. The leader properly chooses the goal because he is responsible for working with it. The validity of the chosen Goal as Understood is always checked with the expert, but *how* the leader does this can be important. In the fullness of their knowledge, experts will make judgments about the *possibility* of a goal and, if they believe it is impossible, will try to keep the group from attempting it. In checking with the expert, the leader should take this natural tendency into account by saying, in effect, "If we can do this, will it make you happy?"

Before moving to the next step, the leader asks the members to put the problem out of their minds and to concentrate on doing what he asks. He is going to take them on a mental Excursion.

People have varying degrees of difficulty learning to put goals (or problems) out of their conscious minds. Literal-minded, accuracy-conditioned people have trouble learning this knack. Those who are less rigorously conditioned to immediate physical consequence of errors find it easier. A physicist or production manager thus usually has more trouble than a poet or writer or psychologist. It is a discipline and a skill much like learning to ride a bicycle. With some effort it suddenly comes to you, and you have little trouble after that.

The *Leader's Question* (abbreviated LQ) begins the Excursion. This is a question that requires an analogical or metaphorical response. Leader's Questions produce metaphorical thinking, which is valuable in achieving creative solutions, by encouraging the mind of each group member to venture into areas seemingly irrelevant to the problem. By focusing attention *away* from the goal (or problem), you increase the probability of viewing the problem in unhabitual, new contexts when you come back to it with the responses. There are three types of Leader's Questions, and these produce three different kinds of analogy: Example, Personal Analogy, and Book Title.

An *Example* (abbreviated EX) is a direct comparison of parallel facts, knowledge, or technology. The procedure requires searching your experience and knowledge for some phenomenon that is similar to the subject at hand. For instance, one Example of closure is a door, another is a mental block. We find that the Examples most likely to achieve their purpose have a common combination of characteristics: the stranger the Example, the more logical distance there is between the subject and the Example, and the more difficult it is to make the Example seem relevant, the greater the chance that it will lead to a new line of speculation. "Mental block" has these characteristics and is more valuable than "door." You are more likely to see a closure problem from a new standpoint if you look at how mental block prevents passage of a memory than if you study the more familiar door.

Examination (abbreviated EXAM). After the leader chooses one of the Examples offered by the group it is desirable to examine the selected Example to produce factual and associatory material, which you will use later to see the problem in a new way. The leader uses three criteria in his choice of an Example for Examination: he finds it interesting, it seems strange and irrelevant to the problem, he believes there is some knowledge about the Example in the group.

We differentiate the facts produced in an Examination. Simple descriptive facts about the Example—for example, "a mental block is invisible"—and superfacts. These are more associatory and speculative statements about the Example—for example, "at some level a mental block is willful, it is protective and exercises foresight, it has its antenna out." Superfacts tends to be more interesting, evocative, and useful than simple facts.

You must learn to involve yourself in the Examination and *not* think back to the problem until asked to do so by the leader. This self-discipline is difficult but important. You must even try not to think back to the Leader's Question that produced the Example. Each step in the Excursion closes the door on the previous step, thus freeing you from thinking of the analogies in any limited way. For instance, in the Examination of a mental block, you should not confine your thinking of it to a closure. The Leader's Question that produced the Example is to be forgotten, and all aspects of mental block are open for exploration. By closing the door after each step, you increase the chances for diversity.

The *Book Title* (abbreviated BT) mechanism, like the Example, helps take a more interesting and therefore better vacation from the problem. In form, a Book Title is a two-word phrase that captures both an essence of and a paradox involved in a particular thing or set of feelings. The combination of an adjective and a noun is the most workable form. The usual purpose of a Book Title is to generalize about a particular and then use it to suggest another Example. This procedure also helps hard-case stay-on-the-problem types get away from the problem. Here is an excerpt from a session. The Example under Examination here was "ratchet":

Lew: A ratchet is a one-way gear; the gear teeth are slanted so that a pawl will slip up one side, but if the gear starts to slip back, the pawl grabs the steep side of the tooth and halts the action.

Carl: It's consistent and it's dependable; very permissive, too, about letting things move in the approved direction. But if you try to go wrong, it stops you short.

Lew: I see it as a mechanical one-way street.

Bill: The pawl that is slipping over the gear teeth might have the feeling of insecurity because it's permitted to click on by, but it learns that the teeth can be relied on as soon as it tries to go the other way. Also, you use a ratchet wrench when there's not enough space to swing the wrench all the way around. You rotate the wrench as far as you can, then back up and let the ratchet click, then go on to move the bolt some more.

Leader: OK, let's move with this. My Question now is for a Book Title. How can we capture an essence of the ratchet, and also have a paradox in it?

You consider the whole ratchet idea from your own point of view. You may use or ignore the material written up. You ask yourself, "What is the essence of those properties or characteristics which are indispensable to this thing (or act or idea), this ratchet?" A number of thoughts might occur to you: dependability, permissiveness, looseness. You select the one that seems to be the most essential. Let's say you pick dependability. Then you ask, "What is paradoxical about a ratchet?" (something opposed to or contradictory to dependability). A number of thoughts may occur: intermittent (from the idea of stop-and-go), controlled, directed, restricted. Now you put some of these thoughts together, taking liberties with proper English if you wish, but striving for something that is aesthetically pleasing, surprising, even poetic.

> Carl: How about Dependable Intermittency?
> Lew: And Directed Permissiveness?
> Bill: What about Permissive One-Wayness?

The first suggestion—Dependable Intermittency—appealed most to the leader. He then asked the group to forget where the Book Title had come from, to close the door on that step of the Excursion and to concentrate on his new Question. By forgetting the source of the Book Title, the group members can make the most of the Book Title's generality.

> Leader: My Question now is for an Example from the world of nature of dependable intermittency.

The Examples suggested were: Old Faithful, changing seasons, tides, conception, and rain.

Personal Analogy (abbreviated PA). This is the third mechanism for developing material to help view the problem in a strange, new context. There are three degrees of involvement in Personal Analogy:

1. First-person description of facts

Leader's Question (Personal Analogy): You are a tuning
   fork. How do you feel?
Response: I am made of metal and have very precise dimen-
   sions. When struck, I vibrate at a fixed frequency.

This is a shallow Personal Analogy, for it gives only
analytical facts, recited in the first person.

2. First-person description of emotions

Leader's Question (Personal Analogy): You are a tuning
   fork. How do you feel?
Response: I feel sensitive but only to very special things.
   You can hit me with a hammer and I don't care at all,
   but if you whistle just the right note, I feel I am going
   all to pieces.

This is a good translation of analytical facts into feelings.

3. Empathic identification with the subject

Leader's Question (Personal Analogy): You are a tuning
   fork. How do you feel?
Response: My nerves are shot. Here I am, a high-grade piece
   of steel, and when the right tone sounds, I have a breakdown! But I am intensely responsible and narrow-
   minded. Dead to anything until *my* frequency comes
   around and then WOW!

We find the third response to be the most interesting
and suggestive. Response to a Personal Analogy is a matter
of degree. You should always press toward empathic involvement. It is best to try to become the thing, and then
to see what your feelings are. What we are suggesting
here is more than the familiar concept of role playing.
Most of us use that type of analogy at one time or another,
"If I were Harry, I would . . ." Role playing seldom produces surprising material and should thus be avoided.
You can use the responses from Personal Analogies in

several ways, including pump priming material for a Book Title. The empathic, emotional responses of Personal Analogy have a vastly different quality than those that come from an Examination. The mechanism of analogy capitalizes on the personal uniqueness of each member of the group, and the usually conflicting emotions that come out help to supply the paradox sought in the Book Title. In addition, Personal Analogy can help to loosen individuals and cohere a team of problem solvers. To become a hatchet or a virus is mentally loosening and broadening. To the degree that you are able to be personal and spontaneous, the experience helps both you and the group to see new things. Although we do not understand the reason, it seems that a group is able to work together more effectively after they have struggled to produce good Personal Analogies. Perhaps when you are new to the method you feel that identifying with a fireplug is about as crazy as you can get; you then feel easier about the other mechanisms.

Force Fit (abbreviated FF) is the most difficult of the Synectics procedures, for it is here that you must take the metaphorical material that has been developed and, in spite of its seeming irrelevance to the problem, force it to be useful. Of the many examples that are available, one recent one will serve to illustrate:

A flash of inspiration can burst out anywhere. For Archimedes it came in the bathtub, and for Isaac Newton beneath an apple tree. But for Britain's Alastair Pilkington, a rangy Cambridge-trained engineer, it came one misty October evening twelve years ago while he was washing the dinner dishes in his two-story brick home outside St. Helens in northwest England.

Pilkington, the production chief and a distant cousin of the founder of the 138-year-old St. Helens glassmaking firm of Pilkington Brothers, Ltd., had been puzzling about a way to produce distortion-free flat glass. Plate glass, the prime type of flat glass, conventionally has been made by running molten glass through rollers and then grinding and polishing away the imperfections. As he scrubbed the dishes that night, Pilkington, staring at the soap and grease floating in the dishwater, suddenly conceived of float glass—an idea that has begun to revolutionize the 5,000-year-old craft of glassmaking. "It was one of those rare moments," Pilkington, now 44, recalled last week, when "the mind is free of all complications and extraneous matters."

Pilkington's idea, refined in thousands of experiments before it was perfected in 1959, was to make glass far more simply and cheaply by floating it in an oven on a bath of molten tin. Then, as the oven is cooled, the glass, hardening before the tin does, can be rolled into the annealing chamber without damaging its brilliant, fire-polished finish. Thus, the costly grinding and polishing steps required for plate glass are eliminated . . . the float-glass price should be reduced, since it costs about 30 percent less to produce than plate glass when a plant is working at full efficiency.[1]

When we have seen the float-glass solution, the soap and grease floating on the water seem quite relevant to the problem. Before Pilkington forced the connection, however, there seemed to be no sensible connection at all.

We have found useful four general approaches to Force Fit. Do not take each specific approach too literally or use it to the exclusion of all the others.

The first approach is a *happening*. Something in the proceedings sparks an idea or an association in your mind. The igniter may be an Example, or a particular piece of the Examination; or it may seem to come from nowhere. For instance, take the following Goal as Understood: Devise a liquid cake icing that will firm up when released from a pressure can. The step preceding Force Fit was the Examination of coal:

1. Turns into diamonds when under pressure.
2. Basically a very simple molecule.
3. Multiple kinds of value; there's the fuel value, which is

[1] *Newsweek*, November 23, 1964. Copyright © 1964 by Newsweek, Inc. Reprinted by permission.

a kind of working value, and then there's the artificial value of the jewels, which is based partly on aesthetic appreciation.

4. The real value comes from difficulty in mining—all the tragedies associated with coal mining, like cave-ins, and slides, and of course all those West Virginia coal miners who are unemployed.

5. Also, those miners lead socially deprived lives; they never see the sun, and they breathe that awful air all day.

At this point the leader chose to go into Force Fit. He followed the usual procedure:

> Leader (*assuming his team has been on vacation and has forgotten the problem*): Let's go into Force Fit. Our GAU is: Devise a liquid cake icing that will firm up when released from a pressure can. How can we use this idea of coal to help us?

The leader deliberately leaves all avenues open. He is then silently watchful, hoping that some member will make a start. In a happening, a member has an association, *feels* it may be helpful, and begins:

> Tom: You know what coal makes me think of? The thing it brings to mind is the grimy coal miner with the lamp on his head. It just seems to me that . . . if . . . on top of our can we have a coal miner's lamp, which doesn't turn on in the refrigerator because it's too cold, but somehow the lamp on the top of the nozzle emits a radiation when it is in the room. This radiation would be of such frequency that some sensitive chemical would congeal and would give us the texture we want.

This start of an idea had nothing really to do with any one piece of the Examination; it came directly from association with the whole Example. It is not a complete idea, but the leader treats it as a valid beginning. He supports it by repeating it and asks the group for help.

Leader: OK, we've got this magic lamp on top of the can. It zaps the liquid and changes it into a solid. How can we make it work?

Sam: Could we turn Tom's lamp into a paddle wheel that beats the liquid icing and whips it so it gets solid?

John: Make it a vibration. . . . Let's see. . . . Could we add air which we vibrate . . . ?

Leader *(supporting)*: Sure—there must be a way of adding air and we have the aerosol power for making vibration. . . . How can we put these together?

Ralph *(the expert)*: You know, that might work. . . . I like that vibration because it really could develop solidity.

And with continuing support from the group Ralph presses toward a Viewpoint. This quick train of associations to the Example has triggered a beginning line of speculation. The important characteristic of a happening Force Fit is that no particular line of thought is suggested by the leader. He does not care where the beginning idea comes from as long as it starts the group toward a Viewpoint.

The second approach to Force Fit is used by the leader when he is in one of these situations:

He gets no response from his team with the happening approach.

After a possible solution is developed and written up.

When the group's attempt to develop a Viewpoint does not succeed.

The leader wants to draw the group back into the material they have developed. He selects a statement from the Examination and attempts to make some loose connections. As he speaks, he is watching his team, hoping they will take the play away from him. As soon as one member speaks, he drops his line of thought and supports the group member's beginning line of speculation:

Leader *(pointing):* Let's take this artificial value idea. . . .
(making it up as he goes) Could we form a cartel like
. . . De Beers . . . and somehow ration out . . .

John *(interrupting):* Look—nothing says we have to make
this happen instantly. Let's put something artificial in
the liquid. When it gets out of the can it grows and
changes. . . .

Leader: You mean your something gradually changes the
liquid into icing right on the cake? I really like the
sound of that idea. How could we . . .

And the group tries to build toward a Viewpoint.

The third approach to Force Fit, the *forced metaphor*,
has four steps and a more structured treatment of the
material. Such a procedure is used if no directions of
speculation occur in the first two attempts.

1. The first step is a conscious consideration of the elements
of the two things we are trying to Force Fit, coal mining
and firming a liquid.

Leader: Well, let's look at a coal mine. What are the elements?

As members of the team tell him, he draws them on the
board for all to see.

Sam: You sink a shaft and there is an elevator in it. The
miners ride down in it and the coal rides up.

John: You have veins of coal going out from the shaft, and
the miners use their tools to chop out those veins.

Leader: OK, let's think of a normal aerosol can with our
liquid icing in it. . . .

Ralph: You have a dip tube and actuating valve . . .

Tom: And nozzle . . .

Leader *(draws):* Now, what is the connection?

The connection, at first, is static—it requires no Force
Fit. It is an attempt to see a relationship.

Harry: Maybe the miner is the dip tube, and the vein of coal he's trying to find and hacks away at is . . . maybe some solid in the can. . . .

The group goes on to connect the elements.

Ralph: What does the nozzle correspond to, I wonder? The elevator?

The group speculates like this and puts up a parallel structure, recognizing that they can always shift the elements if they change their minds. The result is a comparison between a coal mine and an aerosol can full of liquid cake icing.

2. The next step is to make a dynamic connection. This is the meaning of the story. The first step was static, but potentially suggestive. .

Leader: What is the moral of this story for us?
Tom: Maybe the secret is in what happens inside the dip tube, like what happens in the elevator as it goes down and up.

3. The third step is an attempt to free the group from real-world restrictions and to encourage them to speculate wildly but in relation to the problem. Leader: "If you had all the money in the world, and omnipotent powers how would we make Dick's idea work?"

Leader: What could the elevator be, that goes down empty and comes up full, or goes in with people and comes out with coal?
Sam: You know, let's make this a double can. It's one of those dual-component cans, so that there is a chamber of solids, and each time your elevator goes down, it carries with it a piece of that second chamber, just a very small amount of that stuff to interact with the liquid in the other chamber. It puts in a small quantity of solid. There's an interaction as it goes up the tube, and it comes out solid.

Ralph: You know, Jell-O starts out as a liquid and then firms up; doesn't that work by changing the molecular structure somehow?

John: What if we had some radioactive material like plutonium and used it to convert the molecules of the liquid icing into long-chain polymers? That would make it set up the way we want.

4. The final step then is to find some feasible way of making the new idea work. After this you either write the idea up as a Viewpoint, discard it and go off in another direction of speculation, or use it as the Goal as Understood for a new Excursion.

Sam: Isn't there some stuff they use to mix with milk to whip it like cream?

Ralph *(the expert)*: Sure. We could replace the atomic material with CMC (a chemical thickening agent). Then we could have some sort of double delivery system, where the two components of CMC and liquid icing would meet at the nozzle's head. They mix, and out comes our whipped icing.

The *get-fired technique* is a fourth approach to Force Fit that overcomes a difficulty many people have: they are able to develop splendid metaphors while on the Excursion, but as soon as the leader mentions Force Fit, they abandon their free-form thinking and the real-world restrictions quickly take over. The group loses the benefit of the suggestive, diverse material of the Excursion by shifting to a concrete, literal stance that immediately demands a workable solution. This eliminates the period of floating speculation and reduces the chances of producing a new approach. At Force Fit time, you must deliberately delay your return to reality and emphasize dreaming and associatory thinking. Relax with the knowledge that this state is temporary.

The following technique helps accustom you to this sort of thinking: For the first step, take a couple of minutes and write your own Force Fit, which must comply with one rule. The idea you develop must be so outrageous and such a violation of common sense and company policy that when you present it to your boss he will immediately want to fire you.

> Tom: I am going to hire an out-of-work West Virginia coal miner—a very small one—and put one in each can. When the housewife presses the valve, he goes to work.

The restriction introduced has to be absurd—no sensible specifications will do—because the process of staying loose, speculative, and metaphorically minded early in the Force Fit is difficult. The reality (and seriousness) of the problem makes it so. The enforced craziness furnishes a rationale for this playful behavior.

As a second step, you begin to move toward reality. You do this yourself and with the group's help. For example,

> John: You know, Tom, we might build in your coal miner— we could coat the dip tube with something that erodes . . . you know, kind of wears off as the liquid flows past.

The first piece of reality is thus pressed into the wild speculation, and from then on you build, adding more and more reality as you go, until you reach an acceptable Viewpoint or you find the idea unworkable.

The most important aspect of the get-fired procedure is its loosening quality. We have found it particularly valuable in teaching. The trainer takes the leader's role and asks each member to write down his absurd Force Fit in order to get the feeling of stretching the mind. The trainer then asks the group to take a member's absurd idea and turn it into a Viewpoint. This gives members the feel of what it is to support and strengthen an unacceptable and possibly shocking idea into usefulness. This is repeated until the absurdities (and the team members) are exhausted.

Excursion is the term we use describing the Synectics procedure from selection of Goal as Understood through Examination. The Excursion is the artificial vacation referred to earlier.

Synectics is useful in most problem-solving situations including *people problems*; that is, when the problem is people-oriented rather than thing-oriented, Viewpoints are more diffuse and Force Fit more demanding. A *thing problem* has as its objective the development of a device or system, such as inventing a new closure for a thermos bottle. A people problem usually has as its objective the development of a change in behavior, such as motivating bench chemists to make greater innovative contributions to the company. Quite often you will encounter problems that include both people and things, such as devising a system that constantly reminds people to drive automobiles more safely.

When attacking a people problem, you must recognize one particular complication: since everyone is a person, you have a roomful of experts. One person may be responsible for the specific problem, but everyone will have had experiences somehow similar to the problem, and their feelings and opinions about these experiences are strong. The leader must, therefore, take these emotions into account and invite the members to express them in a way that will help, not hinder, the problem-solving process.

Below is a condensed series of meetings concerning a people problem. The differences will be emphasized.

Problem as Given: How can we deal with a senior executive who destroys ideas with vicious pleasure. *(You can detect some subjective response in the words chosen by the expert.)*

Leader: Without mentioning names could you tell us more about your problem?

Tim: Mr. X, who has to approve all the major projects of this department, is a very negative guy. I swear he enjoys proving to you that your idea is not only half-baked but that you are incompetent for proposing it.

Rick: I think the only way to handle him is to get B.J. *(the president)* working on him.

Larry: Have B.J. there a few times to see what X does. . . .

Ralph: The obvious solution is to fire X.

(Laughter.)

Leader: Let's look at that. Could we or should we fire X? . . . I mean, should we seriously conspire and so forth?

Rick: Now let's see . . . where else can I get a job fast . . . ?

Leader: Come on—it isn't a crime to think about this. Besides, everyone is sworn to secrecy *(laughter)*.

The leader is doing two things: first, he is inviting the group to consider the unthinkable and to get it out in the open. Second, he wants them to begin to work within their capabilities. In problems of this sort, the group often spends considerable time venting gripes. The leader will save time by exploring these and pursuing them to their conclusions so that these conclusions can be evaluated. In this case, X could not be fired by the group working on the problem. It might have been possible to make his position difficult.

Larry: Even if we could fire X, I don't think I'd do it. He is a smart guy.

Tim: Yeah! That's what makes him such a ——.

Larry: I mean, look at some of the things he has done. Where would Parts Division be if he hadn't pulled it out?

Leader: How about this idea of Larry's to use B.J. as a moderator or something?

Tim: I'm afraid B.J. . . .

Leader: What do you like about it, Tim?

Tim *(laughingly)*: Well, what I like about it is that B.J. is very sensitive to negativity and he would see what X is doing to projects. Also, X might be more careful with B.J. there. The trouble I see is that probably B.J. already knows that X behaves this way and he doesn't know how to cure it . . . or in his position, he doesn't have to cure it.

Leader: This idea of a third party is appealing—can we turn it into something?

Rick: That third party better have power!

Leader: We are back to B.J.

Larry: How about this: we record the Spectrum Policy and put a speaker under his pillow every night.

(Laughter.)

Leader: Any other suggestions? OK, let's get some goals down.

(The group writes Goals as Understood)

1. How can we force X to use his brightness to help rather than hurt ideas?
2. How can we use a third party to teach X to respond more constructively?
3. Devise a method of presentation that forces X to participate before he judges.
4. How can we make X so secure he can lift our idea up rather than put it down?
5. How can we make every idea belong to X so he will treat it better?

Leader: Now, put the problem out of your mind and go with me. I'm selecting GAU number 2. *(Writes: GAU #2, Leader's Question: Example. Example—Physics— third party influencing.)* From the world of physics give me some Examples of a third party influencing something.

Rick: A fulcrum!

Leader *(writes fulcrum)*: Go ahead, Rick.

Rick: With a lever and a stone, say—you want to move the stone and the two elements are the stone and you and the lever . . . that's three . . .

Leader: That's OK.

Rick: Well, the fulcrum . . . where you place it . . . has an influence on whether you move the stone.

Leader: You and the lever want to move the stone. The point where you balance the lever really decides how much you have to push?

Rick: Yes, and if you put the fulcrum too near you, you may not be able to move the stone at all.

Leader: I think I'm with you. Any other Examples?

Ralph: A wedge!

Leader *(writes it up):* Yes?

Ralph: A wedge is a very simple but subtle tool. The point pierces when you hit the back. But as you drive it in, the force that really matters comes from the fact that the wedge gets thicker. . . .

Leader: Yes. The wedge makes a very small beginning, but once it begins to move in, its shoulders exert gradual but tremendous forces outward?

Ralph: Yeah.

Leader: Let's go with this wedge. *(Writes: LQ:BT: Wedge. Essence and paradox of wedge.)* Let's see if we can put together a Book Title that captures an essence of wedge and contains a paradox.

Tim: How about Gentle Bludgeon?

Leader *(writes it):* What are you thinking, Tim?

Tim: A wedge starts out in a small way . . . almost gently, but once in, it really muscles its way . . . never mind persuasion.

Leader: Can we get a more general word than bludgeon— this is a great idea. . . .

Ralph: Persuader?

Leader *(writes it):* I can see the essence. Can we get more paradox?

Rick: Gentle Explosion.

(Leader writes it up.)

Larry: Piercing Bluntness.

(Leader writes it up.)

Tim: Gradual Extremeness.

(Leader writes it up.)

Ralph: Gradual Cataclysm.

Rick: Compassionate Destruction.

Leader: OK! Enough! *(Writes them up.)*

Tim: Subtle Confrontation.

Leader *(writes):* OK, OK. Let's take one and go. *(Writes: LQ:EX: from geology—example of gradual cataclysm.)* From the world of geology can you think of examples of gradual cataclysm?

Ralph: Drowning coastline.

Leader *(writes it):* Yes?

Ralph: Parts of the continent are slowly getting lower—like Maine, I think. It takes a long time, but it has a huge effect . . . maybe like Atlantis.

Leader: If I get you, some coasts are moving down and the sea is moving inland and sometimes it submerges . . . sometimes it will drown cities and the works. . . .

Ralph: Yeah.

Rick: Erosion.

Leader *(writes it):* Yes, Rick.

Rick: The wind and rain gradually work on a huge mountain . . . and rivers work on it, too. . . . In the end it has disappeared downstream.

Leader: That idea . . . downstream *(laughing).* The mountain looks indestructible, but wind and water work on it gradually and a few million years later it's gone?

Rick: Yes.

Leader *(writes: Examination—erosion):* Let's take that and examine it. Erosion—any thoughts on it?

Rick: In a funny way it's a renewal . . . tough on the mountain but good for the delta.

(Leader writes up as much as possible.)

Larry: It hates the status quo . . . erosion wants to change anything that is there.

Tim: I think of how tireless it is . . . you know, patient. It may be lonely, too. That wind doesn't care if it takes a million years. . . . A grain a day keeps the doctor away. . . .

Ralph: You know erosion uses the mountain itself to break itself down. The wind bounces sand against the rock, the river rolls boulders around, smashing up the mountains. . . .

Leader: Fine! Let's go into Force Fit. *(Writes: Force Fit.)* The problem is, How can we use a third party to teach X to respond more constructively? . . . How can we use this material, this idea of erosion, to help us?

Larry: It makes me think of that saying "Don't let the bastards wear you down."

Leader: Can we think of some way to keep X from wearing us down?

Rick: How about wearing *him* down? There are more of us.

Leader: OK, we outnumber him. How can we wear him down?

Tim *(laughingly):* I can see it now: all five of us take the same idea but we present it differently. I go in and he shoots me down. Rick goes in after I'm through and presents his version. After he's shot down and dragged out, Larry goes in with his version.

(Laughter.)

Leader: How about that? Can we use this, Tim?

Tim: Well, what I like about it is that X would have to repeatedly drag out reasons why the proposal was no good, and he might become aware of his negativity. . . .

Rick: Wait, Tim! Suppose you present your idea and he shoots it down. You come back and give us his negatives. We repair the negatives and you or I or someone . . . better be you . . . take it back and say, "Mr. X, those suggestions you made *(laughter)* . . . now we have incorporated your suggestions in the proposal. Do you think it might work?"

Leader: It sounds like there is something here. . . . What worries you, Tim?

Tim: Getting fired.

Leader: Let's assume we can do this constructively so X really does contribute.

Ralph: I see this as a possibility—we make our proposal loose and deliberately use X's negative comments to build more strength into it. If he gives it the blanket sarcasm treatment, we ask him if he could make his comments more specific so as to help us.

Tim: You sound like a saint.

Leader: No one said it was going to be easy—but it isn't easy now, either. Can we use this, Tim?

Tim: It's sure worth a try.

Leader: OK, how do I write it up?

Tim: Make proposals to X very loose. Present to X and invite his negatives. Work on these weak spots and presents again to X.

(Leader writes it under "Viewpoints" as "#1.")

Rick: Are we ready?

Leader: Yes, fire two!

Rick: Going back to the thought of renewal . . . X needs renewal, and if we keep using his negative comments as positive aids, maybe he will feel better and behave better.

(An untrained group might believe that Rick's suggestion is a Viewpoint, but it lacks concreteness. We call it a Motherhood statement. Everyone can happily agree that it would be fine to renew X, but while there may be the start of a Viewpoint in Rick's statement, there is not enough to design a "Renewal of X" experiment. Notice how the leader presses for specifics.)

Leader: I sure agree that X needs some renewal, and if negative responses are materials we can use, X gives us plenty! How can we renew X with his own negativity?

Larry: I am hooked on Tim's picture of all five of us trooping in one after the other . . . like the boulders in the stream, bouncing off X and staggering out. . . .

Tim: You know, X is a different person when he is dealing with a group—have you noticed, Larry?

Larry: Yes, he is. It's almost as though he has an audience and he has an image of how he should behave. Not that he isn't pretty negative still. . . .

Leader: Are you guys building on Rick's thought of using X's negative . . . ?

Rick: Hey! What are they saying? Let's use this characteristic of X's . . . he treats three people better than one . . . let's always present proposals in a body of three!

Leader: That's fascinating. What do you think, Tim?

Tim: Absolutely! It is so obvious!

Leader: What shall I write?

Tim: Always make proposals to X with three people present.

Leader (writes it as "Viewpoint #2"): Good! Let's go back to Rick's idea of using his own negativity to help X renew himself.

People problems are often vague and invite general speculation. It is so easy for the group to become philosophical and produce observations that are not good material for experiment that the leader must be alert and insist that the group keep pressing Motherhood statements toward specific procedures.

Ralph: You see that idea of patience up there? Well, if someone could be that patient with X—stay with him all day long and not, you know, say, "Now, now, mustn't" every time X is negative but just reflect it to him—maybe in a million years . . .

Leader: That would be an example of using X's momentum to help him. Can we think of some way to make this happen?

Rick: Let's use the three guys!

Leader: Yes, let's use them. . . .

Rick: Say it's Tim, Ralph, and me . . . one, two, three. One presents the idea. X points out a flaw. Two picks it up and repeats the negative thinking to make sure everyone understands it and to make sure it's visible to X. Next negative is picked up by three.

Tim: I like that! And one, two, and three could use the same opening words like, "Mr. X, if I understand, you don't believe this will work because . . ."

Rick: Maybe they use the same monotonous tone of voice.

Ralph: And maybe we should all have an application in for another job.

Tim: I think Ralph has a point. I like the idea of having some sort of signal that ties the negatives together, but X is no fool, and I am concerned about laying it on too thick.

Leader: Tim, do you think careful feedback by one after another is worth trying?

Tim: Yes, I do. (*Writes: Group of three, in turn, listens to and repeats X's negative statements, hoping he will become more aware of what he is doing.*)

(*Leader writes it as "Viewpoint #3."*)

Larry: As you were saying, Tim, X is no fool. When he reacts negatively and one, two, or three feeds back, maybe the others can try building . . . try the Spectrum Policy. Maybe we reverse it at first: you say, in effect, "Yes, there are these things wrong with the idea, but there are these things that are worthwhile—can we build on them?" If X can see how to function helpfully, I believe he would . . . He believes now that it is his job to kill frail ideas so no time is wasted.

Leader: Can we nail this down?

Tim: Yes, and this ties in with our first Viewpoint. Larry is saying that we run a session with X. We use his negatives as starting points—recognize the bad he sees but also emphasize the good and ask his help. We set an example. It is worth trying.

Leader: What shall I write?

(Tim dictates Viewpoint #4.)

Leader: Let's go back to our material. . . .

Ralph: You know, those boulders . . . Erosion does not depend on one boulder; it sends 15,372 to do the job. Shouldn't we give X more than one idea?

Rick: I like that. When we make a presentation to X we should give him more than one alternative to chew on.

Tim: I like that, too. We could give three alternatives and after the one-two-three treatment on each, we choose the one that is least repulsive to X and concentrate on that.

Leader: What do I write?

(Tim dictates Viewpoint #5.)

With people problems the leader and expert must be sensitive to the gradual emergence of a policy. It is beginning to be apparent in the session above. They have called it the "Dealing-with-X Policy," and it is articulated when it can be supported by Viewpoints.

Leader: Tim, are you beginning to see a policy?

Tim: I think so. Let me try it on you guys.

The Dealing-with-X Policy

1. We will always outnumber him.
   a. Never present an idea alone—use a three-to-one ratio.
   b. Present a number of ideas or alternatives; perhaps three is a good number.
   c. We will, in each encounter, call attention to negative reactions as many times as we can.

2. We will try to use X's wits in spite of him and hope he will learn.
   a. We will try to build on his negative points.
   b. We will correct each other in front of him—that is, enforce, with each other, the Spectrum Policy.
   c. We will invite him to help us build.

If such a policy can be developed, it greatly increases the probability that something can be done. A single Viewpoint almost never has the climactic quality of complete solution. You will usually need fifteen or twenty. When they have been woven into a policy, they become easier to remember and to apply consistently.

The policy statement may take different forms. You should feel free to use any unifying device you can invent. A group of bench chemists working on the problem of motivating bench chemists (after all, who could be more expert in the problem?) developed a policy called the "Bill of Rights." It had a preamble with some statements about the company, the individual, and the goals of each. They listed fourteen rights; some were company rights, some individual rights. The Viewpoints were introduced as experiments toward securing one or more rights.

The point is that in the confusion that usually surrounds people problems, it is vital that you give the several Viewpoints coherence. Further, you should always be ready to modify or change the policy as new Viewpoints suggest.

Viewpoint (abbreviated VP). If the Force Fit is successful, a possible solution is developed. We call this a Viewpoint. Viewpoints are not final solutions until they have been made to work. The task of transforming a Viewpoint into a solution should not be underestimated. From our experiments in implementation, in our own company, and in client companies, developing promising Viewpoints is perhaps 5 percent of the job. Implementation is the other 95 percent: the first 5 percent is vital, but difficult hurdles remain.

Creative problem solving is a complicated process. Once you have a Viewpoint worth pursuing, continuing creativity is essential. Probably the Viewpoint will not work as expected. Indeed, by the time a Viewpoint is made into a marketable product or a usable policy, it will have changed considerably. If you know its history, you will see that an end product is a third or fourth cousin to the original Viewpoint. The product would not exist without that Viewpoint, but it owes its life more to the implementation than to the conception.

Since we know that the world is hard on even the best Viewpoints, you must be rigorous before you accept an idea as a Viewpoint. The criteria for evaluating a Viewpoint are:

> The expert must believe the idea has new elements and is promising.
> The expert must know exactly what next steps to take to test its validity.

Finally, an expert should not be sent forth armed with only one Viewpoint. Five are better and ten twice as good. The expert with ten Viewpoints has alternative shoring-up materials. If one Viewpoint shows weaknesses, he can borrow from others or shift to a new one.

You have seen the difference between Viewpoints in thing problems and those in people problems. With things, a single Viewpoint may seem completely new and promise a full solution. With people this is seldom true. Each Viewpoint will usually have elements that are familiar and some that are new. No single Viewpoint is the answer, but ten or fifteen Viewpoints welded into a policy may represent a real innovation in dealing with the Problem as Given.

You have now been introduced to the jargon of Synectics. These terms are useful in helping you to grasp the procedures. In the early stages of learning you may use them a good deal. However, as the mechanics of leading an Excursion become familiar it is desirable to de-emphasize the terminology. As leader, you may write "LQ:EX" on the pad, particularly if the group is unfamiliar with the steps, but your objective is to press the session forward without distractions. While making it completely clear to his team exactly what he wants them to do, a leader should not make too much of the steps.

Early, as the leader, you may write "LQ:EX physics— third party doing something," and you say, "My question is for an Example from the world of physics; please give me Examples of a third party doing something."

Later, as the procedure becomes familiar, you write the same things but you are less formal in your speech: "Can you think of Examples from physics of a third party doing something?"

In general, the less the structure intrudes, the better. You should feel free to experiment to the point of no visible structure. Keep alert for signs of misunderstanding and confusion. These mean that your team is not getting proper direction from you.

6
Directed Originality

Straightforward thinking about a problem usually produces a number of possible solutions. Characteristically, these are not novel but consist of a combination of familiar elements. For instance, suppose a car manufacturer is concerned over the high accident death rate. In modifying the car design, he thinks in terms of things he knows: raise the rear lights to make them more visible, make all interior surfaces energy-absorbing, make the steering wheel collapsible, etc. This is normal and understandable, but it is inhibiting in two ways: first, to stay in old paths tends to invite the mediocre. It is tempting to embellish known solutions rather than speculate in entirely new directions. Second, because all of us are conditioned toward self-preservation, common sense suggests that we stick to the familiar and the possible. Rather than risk discomfort and failure, we tend to set goals we can live with. This prudence or caution eliminates the wild or wishful, the truly innovative goal. British author Arthur C. Clarke has said, "When a distinguished but elderly scientist states that something is possible, he is almost certainly right. When he states that something is impossible, he is very probably wrong."[1] Tom Alexander tells us:

Recent history is full of incidents in which highly knowledgeable individuals have flatly denied the feasibility of some development, which before long turned out to be quite practicable.

[1] Tom Alexander, "The Wild Birds Find a Corporate Roost," p. 130.

For example, the great atomic-theory pioneer, Lord Rutherford, insisted that it was impossible to harness nuclear energy.[2]

It is important to cultivate the attitude that anything is possible.

You have seen how the Goal (Problem) as Understood encourages you to wish for whatever you want. The auto company seeking a safer design might have included among its Goals as Understood "How to integrate the driver so closely with his car that when he behaves recklessly, the car stops for ten minutes." Once you choose a wishful Goal as Understood, using Example, Book Title, and Personal Analogy can help to liberate you from the traditional approach, to escape from rut thinking.

In the following transcript of an automobile safety session, the diagrams show the mind of a group member as he witnesses the Excursion. You can see how the conscious use of metaphor leads you to explore areas of knowledge and experience that would not ordinarily be brought to bear on the problem and increases the probability of perceiving in an unhabitual way.

The diagram (page 122) is of that part of the member's mind containing the knowledge logically related to auto safety. When the subject is brought up or the individual ponders about it, he tends to cycle and recycle this material and never leave the area labeled "Auto Safety."

> GAU: How can the driver be so closely integrated with his car that when he behaves recklessly the car stops for ten minutes?

The expert and other group members are asked to put the problem out of their minds and to concentrate on the Excursion.

> Leader (LQ:EX): From the world of machines give me an Example of an integrated driver or controller.

[2] *Ibid.*

Herb: A governor.
Leader: Yes?
Herb: The governor senses the rpms of an engine; if too slow, it opens the throttle; if too fast, it closes it.

The leader selected the world of machines. Since the problem is people-oriented, he was wise to choose an inorganic world; but the governor example is too close to automobiles, so is the world of machines, and it will be difficult to get the problem out of the forefront of the mind and thus difficult to see it in a new way.[3]

The leader saw his mistake and made a fresh start.

Leader: (LQ:EX): From the world of climatology give an Example of integration.
Herb: Tornado.
Leader: Tell me more, Herb.
Herb: A tornado sucks up and makes part of itself—integrates—cars, haystacks, houses, children; whatever is movable in its path.

The Leader's Question sends the group member's attention and his preconscious to an area of the mind that has no seeming connection with auto safety. Chances are slim that traditional analysis of the facts would ever consciously search this part of the mind.

The conscious mind has put aside the problem and is concentrating on an Example of integration from climatology. The preconscious helps with the search, but never

[3] The importance of developing strangeness in the example has been tested by research on Synectics done by the navy. "In two experiments involving hundreds of solutions to problems, it was found that the solutions based on the strange and apparently irrelevant analogies were more novel (on the average) than solutions based on the more obvious analogies. The sample size for the first experiment (2 problems) was 83 college students, while the sample size for the second experiment (7 problems) was fifty-eight." (Dr. Robert W. Stephenson, U. S. Naval Ordnance Test Station, China Lake, California; unpublished research.)

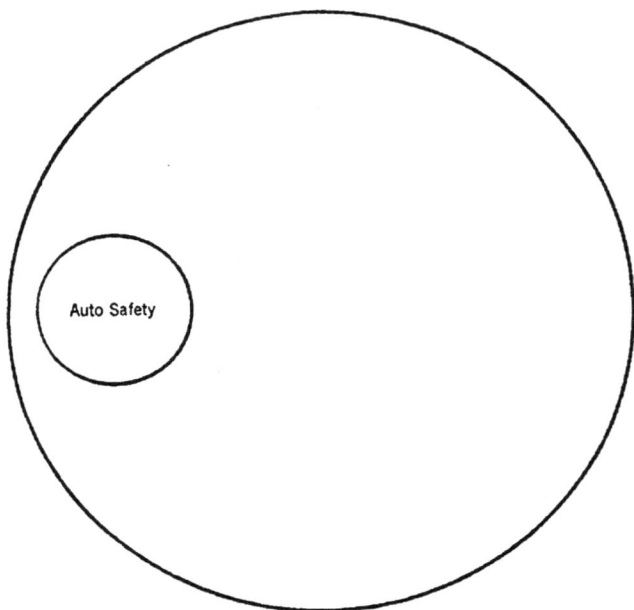

for an instant does it neglect or forget the real problem. All during the search, it picks up half-forgotten bits of knowledge and associations (represented by the bumps on the bold black lines) that *it* feels may be relevant to the GAU or PAG. The conscious mind is not aware of this activity.

Leader: Can you think of a Book Title for "tornado"?
Alan: Indiscriminate Selector.
Leader: What's on your mind?
Alan: A tornado doesn't seem to choose its path, and it seems to pick up the things it does in a random fashion. But the things it does pick up sure know they have been selected for special attention.

Referring to the next figures, the new Leader's Question designated tornado and the part of the brain containing knowledge and associations to that topic. It is as though a small portion of a map were blown up for a

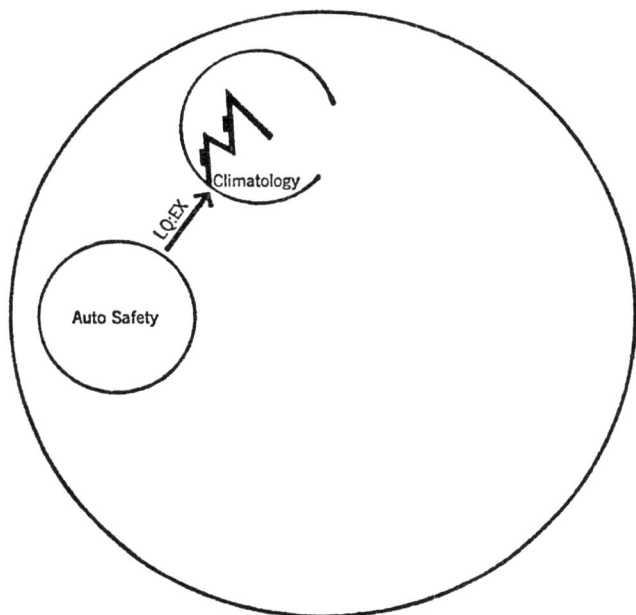

different and more detailed examination. The preconscious continues to collect and retain any material it encounters which *it* considers relevant to the problem.

Leader (LQ:EX): From the world of sonics can you give an Example of Indiscriminate Selector?

Herb: Fire alarm. Everyone can hear it, but it is really designed to signal firemen and select them.

Joe: Tuning fork.

Leader: Tell us more about tuning forks.

Joe: A tuning fork is very precise in the vibrations per second it will give out or respond to, but it is completely indiscriminate about the source of the sound it reacts to.

You will note that the Book Title serves two particularly useful purposes. First, it is a step that very efficiently takes the conscious mind away from the problem and leads to seemingly unconnected areas. Second, it broadens

These blips represent long-forgotten memories that the preconscious scans and then "picks up" as useful clues. For instance, one might be: "When I was three years old a high wind knocked me down. That is not safe."

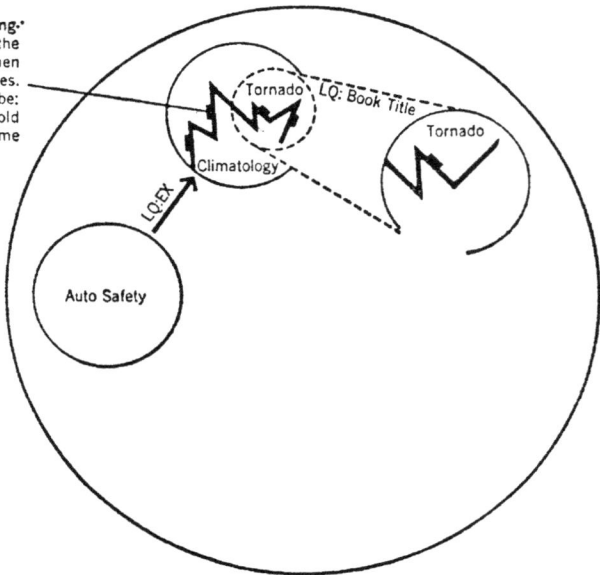

"I dreamed I was in a tornado once. I was safe as long as I stayed in the center."

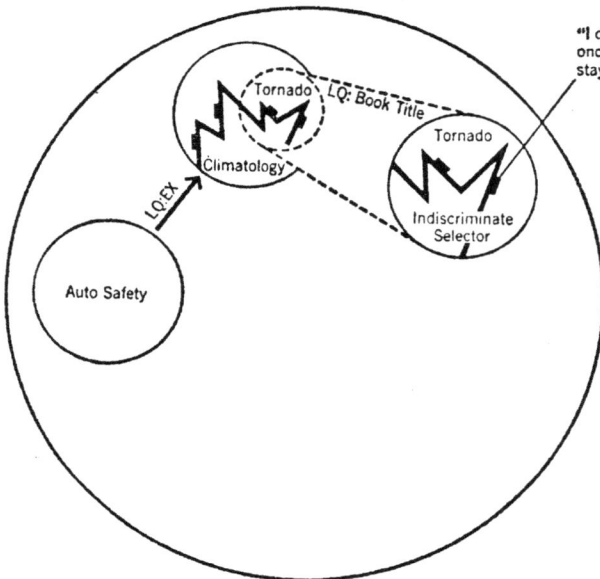

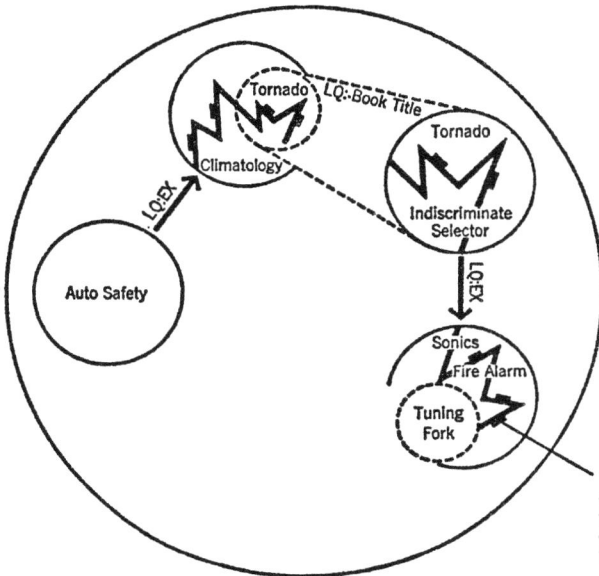

"I remember watching fire engines. You never get in their way. You watch them closely because of the noise they make."

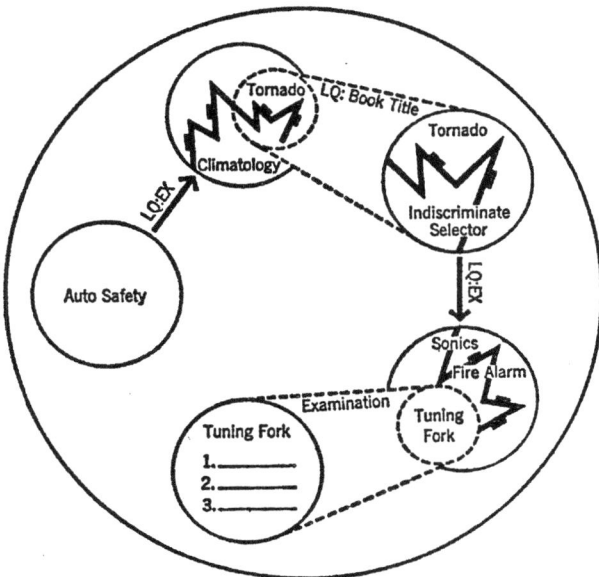

the possible areas of search in the mind. While a good Book Title effectively captures an essence of its subject, it is so general that it also captures an essence of many other things. To continue the above Excursion, the leader selects *tuning fork* for Examination.

Examination: Tuning fork.

Joe: A tuning fork is a kind of detective. If the vibrations it is sensitive to are present in any volume, it begins to jump around.

Herb: It is also a judge or example. If you are tuning a violin or something like that, you bang the right tuning fork and it tells you whether you are right or wrong.

Alan: If you put a vibrating tuning fork in water, it will make visible the sound waves it is sending out.

Note that the material that comes out in the Examination is not necessarily accurate.

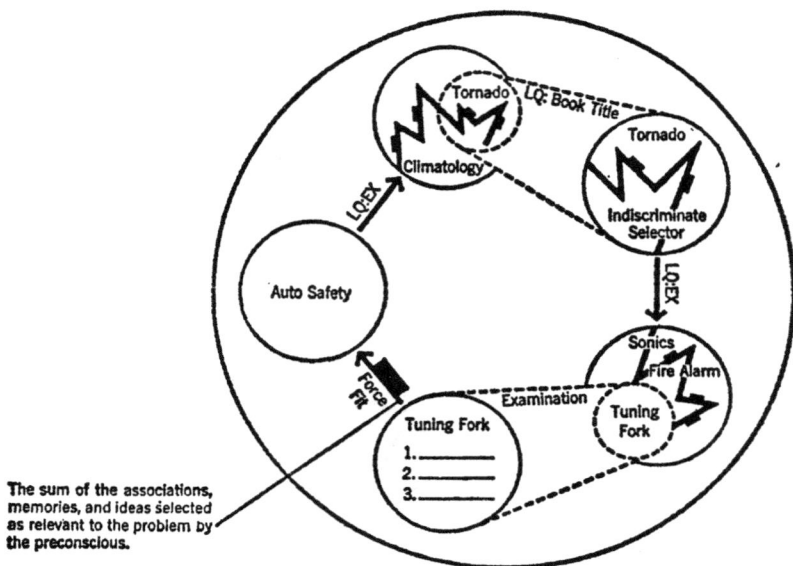

The sum of the associations, memories, and ideas selected as relevant to the problem by the preconscious.

Leader: Let's move into Force Fit: Our problem is how to integrate a driver so closely that when he behaves recklessly the car stops for ten minutes. How can we use the idea of the tuning fork to help us?

At this point the conscious mind comes back to the problem of auto safety and sees it in a strange way by using tuning fork as a context. New lines for speculation come not only from this strange context, but also from the load of clues, associations, and memories brought forward by the preconscious.

Herb: Is there some sonorous, smooth tone that a car has when it is being properly driven? You know, smooth, no raucous noises?

Leader: Herb, are you thinking of a car that acts almost like a cat? You treat him right and he normally purrs. If you treat him wrong—look out! Is there some sound we can use?

Joe: Herb, thinking of your difference between driving and treating the car wrong—suppose we had an oscilloscope sensing the strain on . . . maybe the front axle or the frame. I'll bet a reckless driver puts a lot more strain on a car.

Alan: We have an acceptable strain pattern, and as soon as it is exceeded, the ignition cuts out.

Leader: Maybe we don't need an oscilloscope.

This session eventually led to a practical device for monitoring driving habits. This device is being test-marketed. We hypothesized that a person with bad driving habits would be forced to brake and turn sharply more often than a driver with better habits. Experiments with taxi fleets and teen-age drivers supported the hypothesis. We also found that by making a signal to the driver whenever such a "mistake" occurred he could substantially change his habits.

We have developed three basic kinds of Excursion to bring uninhibited thinking into play.

EXAMPLE EXCURSION

This is the simplest kind of Excursion. The steps from Problem as Given through development of Goals as Understood have been completed. These have helped participants understand the problem both by getting a personal feel for it and by having them imagine a possible solution. Each has done a preliminary search of his experiences for material suggestive to solutions. Chances are good that he is being quite strict with himself about relevance. The purpose of the Excursion is threefold. First we want each participant to search his experiences more widely, we want him to relax his standards of what might be useful, and finally we want him to engage in a playful, cooperative activity with his team members. This third purpose is as important as either of the others. It reinforces the personal-exchange style that insists no one will lose and everyone *can* win.

The progression of thinking from Problem to Possible Solution can be summarized in this flow chart:

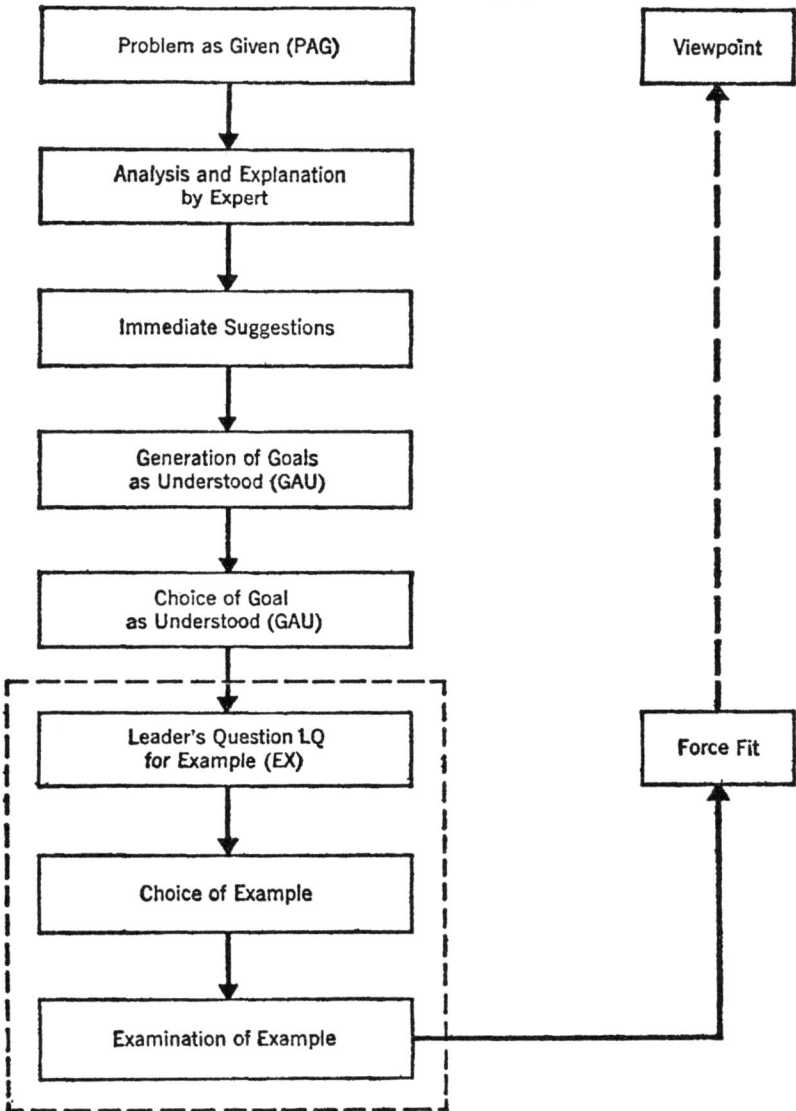

SYNECTICS FLOW CHART
EXAMPLE EXCURSION

Comments

PROBLEM AS GIVEN

Leader writes: PAG: Devise a thermos with an integral closure.

ANALYSIS

See thermos explanation and specifications on page 17.

IMMEDIATE SUGGESTIONS

No further immediate solutions come to mind.

GENERATION OF GOALS AS UNDERSTOOD

1. How can we make a thermos that grows closed when we want it to?

2. Devise an integral mechanism that has learned to open and close on signal.

3. Devise a closure that doesn't take up space.

All these GAUs involve good wishful thinking. We find that practical-minded people are often distressed by a Goal like number 2. They often say, "Let's face it, you can't teach a mechanism anything. This is misleading and sloppy thinking." Strictly speaking, they are right, but our observations suggest that this is not the time for precision. The misleading and sloppy aspects of the statement are often stimu-

Comments

lating and lead away from the familiar paths. Nearly every statement made in a Synectics meeting should be taken loosely, not literally. The time for precision comes in the final evaluation of a possible solution.

Now let us analyze an Example Excursion, concerning the thermos bottle closure problem we have already encountered:

Excursion	*Comments*
CHOICE OF GAU	
Leader chooses GAU—devise a closure that doesn't take up space—and writes: GAU #3.	This last GAU appeals most to the leader.
LEADER'S QUESTION	
Leader: Let's try to get the problem out of our minds. My Question is for an Example.	The leader selects an appropriate key part of the GAU (he does not ask for an Example of the whole problem).
Leader: Please think of an Example of a closure from the world of biology. (*Writes: LQ:EX: From biology—Example of closure.*)	He asks for an Example from the organic world because the problem is a technical one.
Tom: How about a *clam?*	
(*Leader writes: Clam. He asks Tom*): Could you tell us more?	

Excursion   *Comments*

Tom: Well, I always think of a clam as being closed up tighter than almost anything else I know. It's just about impossible to get through without breaking his shell.

Although the Example response may seem obvious to the leader, he still must ask for Tom's explanation. Tom *may* have in mind a connection which would never occur to the leader. In any case, the leader never makes the assumption that he knows what a member is thinking.

Leader: Do you mean it's a very effective closure that you can get through only with a great deal of difficulty?

The leader, by restating *the member's idea* in the leader's own words, proves he has heard and understands.

Tom: Yes.

Leader: Are there any other Examples of closure from biology?

Dick: Natural selection.

(Leader writes it down and says): Yes?

Dick: Natural selection is the gradual closing out of certain physical traits or characteristics, like man's losing his tail or certain ducks' losing their ability to fly.

You will note that during the Example stage, the leader writes very little and listens very hard.

Leader: If I get you, in natural selection a person or animal gradually loses cer-

Now the leader uses his own words to feed back the meaning he has got from Dick.

Excursion *Comments*

tain physical attributes or capabilities, and so in a sense they are closed out of that particular species.

Dick: Exactly; those things are obsolete and are left out of future generations.

Leader: Great! Can anyone think of any other Examples?

James: How about an *iris?*

Leader writes: Iris. He asks James to explain his thought.

James: I was thinking about the iris in your eye. I don't know too much about this, but it seems to me the iris closes out light and images and things like that.

Leader: Do you mean that, as part of the eye, the iris helps to close out some things you might see?

James: That's right.

CHOICE OF EXAMPLE AND EXAMINATION

Leader: That idea intrigues me. Let's examine it. *(Writes: Examination: Iris.)*

He chooses it (1) because the concept of an iris interests

Excursion   *Comments*

him; (2) he can see no practical connection between eyes and the thermos, and (3) he believes the group knows enough about the iris to examine it.

Leader: What's with this iris?

Leader gets ready to write fast, abbreviating where possible, leaving out nonessential words but always using member's own words.

James: Well, I'm not even sure it's the iris that does this. It's more sort of a vague image I have, and I don't really have any more details about it. Except that it's the colored part.

This Examination is a good example of where an intuition is often more valuable than precise factual knowledge.

Dick: One thing about the iris that I remember is that it contracts and expands—sort of stretchable stuff that makes it possible to open and close.

In this Examination, no one has much precise factual knowledge, but everyone is familiar with the subject and can speculate about it. In this step it is more important to say something interesting than to say something that is correct. There is room here for contradictory views.

Tom: It's funny, but when James said iris the first time, I thought he meant the iris of a camera, the part that's made of lots of metal leaves that fold over one another

Excursion

Comments

to let the light in and expose the film.

James: Also they fold over
each other the most on the
outside parts of the leaves.

This is the sort of associatory
material which can be especially valuable in leading to
new areas of speculation. Remember also that each new
step in the Flow Chart closes
the door on the previous one,
so Tom's thoughts about an
iris are not restricted to
James's idea from the world
of biology.

Dick: There's also the flower,
iris, but I don't know much
about it.

Tom: I keep thinking of the
eyeball. It's a funny, squishy
substance.

FORCE FIT

*Leader writes: Force Fit. He
says:* Let's go into Force
Fit. How can we use these
ideas about the iris to help
us solve the problem of devising a thermos with an integral closure? (He chooses
in this case to focus on
the PAG rather than the
GAU.)

(Silence.)

Leader gives the group time

Excursion   *Comments*

	to speculate and try to attempt a Force Fit.
Leader: Let's take this idea of the leaves. They remind me of the petals of a flower which seem to slide up and close together. Can we get anything from that?	When a group cannot make a connection after thirty or forty seconds, the leader tries to stimulate them.
Dick *(excitedly)*: You mean sort of like the sections of a dome or the bowl of a collapsible flash attachment . . . ?	
Tom: Yeah. I like that idea. I like the way those sections slide back and disappear. How can we keep it from having so many mechanical parts?	Good building by Tom. Notice how he uses the Spectrum Policy: he points out what he likes about Dick's idea, then introduces the mechanical complication but emphasizes that it is the group's problem, not Dick's alone.
James: Dick, you said something about the material of the human eye, that it was stretchable. Is there some way we can make an iris closure out of a stretchable material?	Good listening and building by James. He is still speculating. Notice that he freely credits Dick with starting his thought. This recognition, small as it seems, is important in building mutually enjoyable interdependence. Without this you do not get whole-hearted teamwork.
Tom: Hey, you get that kind of a closure when you twist a long balloon in the middle. You get two separate halves.	

Excursion	*Comments*

Dick: Yeah, and that's an air-
    tight closure.

Tom jumps up and draws a
    diagram.

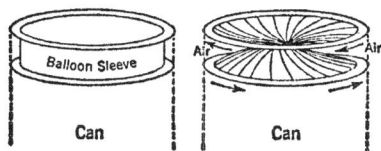

You could do it like this:
    have some rubbery material
    attached at the top and
    bottom, but be able to turn
    the top part, so when you
    do, it closes in the middle
    like a twisted balloon.

The group considered this idea to be a worthwhile
Viewpoint. Subsequent experiments proved that the closure met all the specifications. The figures below illustrate
its operation, fully open, half-open, and closed. It is now
also being marketed as a closure for lipstick cases.

BOOK TITLE EXCURSION

Book Title seems the most foreign and unnatural of the mechanisms of Synectics, but it provides an extra mechanism to take a more effective vacation from the problem. The two-word statement to capture the essence with a paradox is not new. Many book titles, not surprisingly, qualify. Originally we called this stop symbolic analogy and thought of it differently. It developed when we asked team members to characterize a thing (like a closure) in a compressed way. To explain what we wanted we would say, "Pretend you have written a whole book about closures. Think of a two-word, poetic title for your book without the word closure." One title that would qualify: Penetrable Barrier.

Comments

PROBLEM AS GIVEN

(Leader writes: PAG: Devise an ice tray that releases ice without effort.)

ANALYSIS

The ice tray must be superior to anything on the market and must not cost any more than those already available.

IMMEDIATE SUGGESTIONS

Leader: Does anyone have a solution?

Jim: Could you make it out of a very stretchy plastic?

Comments

Have a crank and roller attached to one end. When you want ice you wind the crank and it rolls up the ice tray, dumping out the ice.

Leader *(to expert):* How about that, Harry?

Harry: Sounds good. I've never thought of a roll-up ice tray.

Leader *(Going to Viewpoint sheet):* How shall I put that?

Harry: Stretchy plastic roll-up ice tray.

(Leader so writes.)

GENERATION OF GOALS AS UNDERSTOOD

1. How can we make an ice tray disappear after ice is made?

2. How teach an ice tray to release instantly on signal.

Excursion

CHOICE OF GAU

Leader chooses GAU: How make an ice tray disappear

Excursion   *Comments*

after ice is made. *(Writes GAU #1.)*

EVOCATIVE QUESTION

Leader: My Question is for an Example—please think of an Example from human behavior of disappearing after a function is completed. *(Leader has now written: LQ:EX: From human behavior—Example of disappearing after function is completed.)*

Sam: I can't help thinking of an erection.

Leader: Fine—what about it? *(Writes: Erection.)*

Sam: Well, of course, you have an erection, but after ejaculation it begins to disappear.

Leader: So after the function is completed, the expansion is what disappears. Is that what you meant?

Sam: Yes, that's it.

Leader: Good. Any more Examples?

Harry: How about a kid breaking a window?

SYNECTICS FLOW CHART
BOOK TITLE EXCURSION

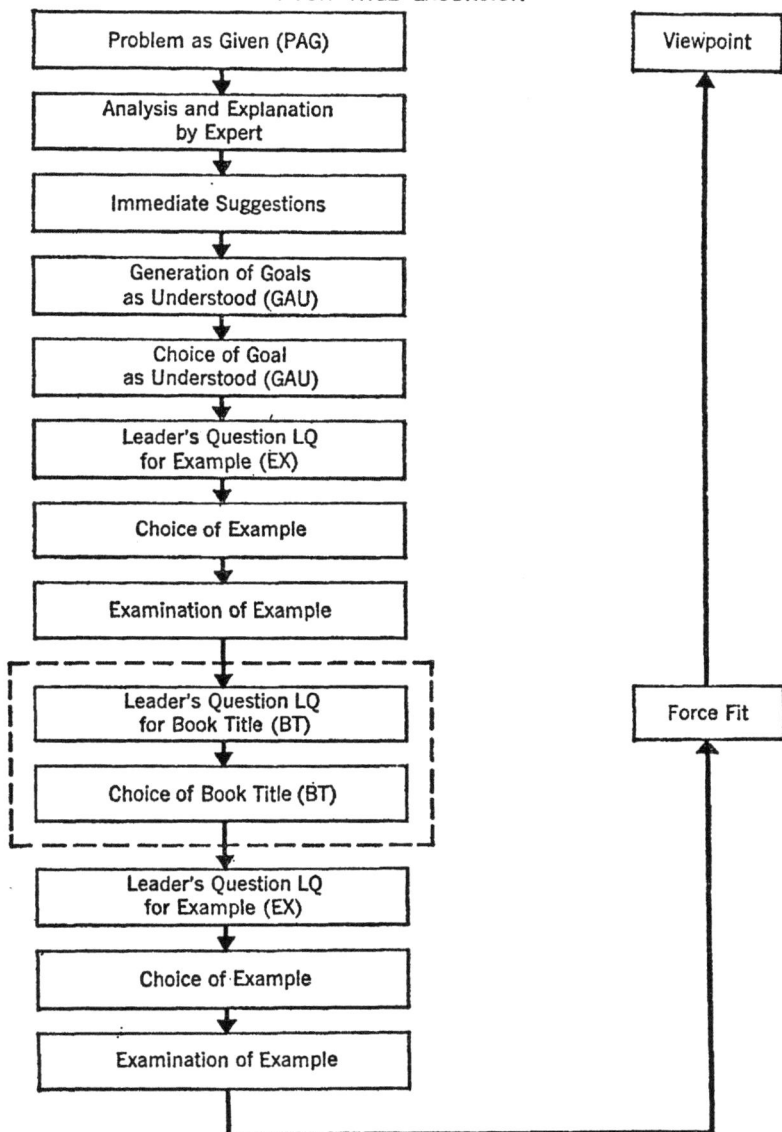

Problem as Given (PAG)

Analysis and Explanation
by Expert

Immediate Suggestions

Generation of Goals
as Understood (GAU)

Choice of Goal
as Understood (GAU)

Leader's Question LQ
for Example (EX)

Choice of Example

Examination of Example

Leader's Question LQ
for Book Title (BT)

Choice of Book Title (BT)

Leader's Question LQ
for Example (EX)

Choice of Example

Examination of Example

Viewpoint

Force Fit

Excursion   *Comments*

(Leader writes: Kid breaking window.): What do you have in mind, Harry?

Harry: Assuming for a moment that a kid's function is to break windows, as soon as it is done, he gets out of there . . . hoping he won't get caught.

Leader: That *is* an important function of kids! For some reason they want to see the window destroyed. Mission accomplished, they run for cover so they won't have to pay a penalty—is that how you meant this?

Harry: That's it.

CHOICE OF EXAMPLE AND EXAMINATION

Leader: Let's go with this kid throwing a rock through a window. *(Leader writes: Examination — Kid — Rock through window.)* Any thoughts about this kid?

Harry: Now that I think of it more carefully, it is a strange activity. . . . The kid knows he is inviting trouble, knows that he is wrong, but he does it anyway. If I ever did it, and

Leader writes fast as Harry speaks.

Excursion   *Comments*

I can't remember, I believe the running away—the escaping—is as exciting as the breaking.

Jim: Usually a kid has some rationalization, you know. People of the house were mean or something, and he says to himself, They deserve this.

Harry: I'll bet a kid will use that sort of rationalization even when it wasn't the people. You know, say his father spanks him . . . then he goes out and breaks the Smiths' picture window.

Jim: Better to take a chance on the Smiths than another whopping from his dad!

Sam: I hate to resort to jargon with you guys, but this displacement of anger is at the bottom of juvenile delinquency.

LEADER'S QUESTION FOR A
BOOK TITLE

Leader: Let's move on. My Question is for a Book Title. How can we capture the essence of his throwing a rock through a window— and have a paradox in it?

Excursion	*Comments*

(Writes: LQ:BT: For Kid—Rock through window: (1) Essence (2) Paradox.)

(There is a pause for thinking.)

1. Each group member considers the whole idea from his own point of view. He may or may not use the material generated in the last step.

2. He asks himself, "What is the essence of those properties or characteristics which are indispensable to this act—the kid throwing a stone through a window?" A number of thoughts might occur, for example.

   a. anger
   b. revenge
   c. hostility
   d. destructiveness
   e. mental disturbance

3. He selects the one that seems to him the most essential. Let's say it is hostility.

4. Now he asks himself, "What is paradoxical about the kid throwing?" etc. He thinks of it in connection

Excursion   *Comments*

with the idea he has se-
lected in number 3 above.
Again   a   number   of
thoughts may occur, for
example:

a. comfort
b. relief (the hostile act
may bring these to the
child)
c. deception
d. falseness (the act may
not be from anger at
the window owner)

5. Now he puts some of
these together; he takes
liberties with proper English if he wishes.

Jim: How about Hostile Comfort?

Leader *(writes it):* How
come?

Jim: The kid, for whatever
reason, is feeling mighty
hostile and angry; when he
smashes that window his
feelings are transformed . . .
somehow he is comforted
or feels excited or something
rather than hostile.

Leader: Very interesting.

Sam: Aggressive Surrender.

Excursion   *Comments*

Leader *(writes it):* You got me, Sam.

Sam: The kid is boiling with aggression about something. Most of the time he keeps it bottled up, but just as he is going by my house, he gives in . . . surrenders and lets fly at my window.

Leader: You sound like you speak from the heart!

Sam: I am a victim.

Jim: Constructive Destruction.

Leader *(writes it):* What are you thinking, Jim:

Jim: Well, the act . . . busting the picture window is harmful . . . destructive . . . but maybe it lets steam out of the kid and he doesn't knife someone.

Leader: Your idea has a lot of allure, but can we think of a less trite way of putting it?

Harry: How about Healthful Destruction.

If the idea behind a trite or poor Book Title is good, the leader asks the member and the rest of the group to help rephrase it.

Excursion   *Comments*

Jim: Knowing Wrongness.

(Leader writes them.)

Sam: Right Wrongness.

Jim: Intelligent Mistake.   Leader has stopped asking for
                                     explanations because the group
                                     is hot. If he needs an explana-
                                     tion, he can go back.

(Leader writes them all.)

Sam: How about Rational
    Emotionalism?

(Leader writes it.)

Harry: Sam, would you buy
    Rational Impetuousness?

(Leader writes it, too.)

Sam: Yeah, that's even better.

Leader: Enough, we have
    some good ones here.

(The list of Book Titles is:

1. *Hostile Comfort*

2. *Aggressive Surrender*

3. *Constructive Destruction*   (Trite)

4. *Healthful Destruction*

5. *Knowing Wrongness*

Excursion	Comments
6. *Right Wrongness*	(Trite)
7. *Intelligent Mistake*	
8. *Rational Emotionalism*	
9. *Rational Impetuousness.)*	

Leader *(after consideration— or immediately if his taste and pleasure dictate):* Let's take Rational Impetuousness.

LEADER'S QUESTION

Leader: My Question is for an Example from the world of nature of rational impetuousness. *(Writes: LQ:EX: Nature—rational impetuousness.)*

The leader, and only he, should mentally refer back to the problem. His goal is to take the group on an excursion away from the problem. If he fails to refer back to the problem and make a conscious attempt to avoid it, he will probably unconsciously favor a Book Title that promises to give a solution. Such selection will lead to solutions but they will have a lower probability of being novel.

Sam: Seed pod.

Leader *(writes it):* Say some more.

The leader moves from Book Title to Example to produce some specifics that will be appropriate for Examination. These Examples, because they come from the generality of the Book Title, will be some steps removed, in strangeness, from the problem.

Sam: I was thinking of those pods that have little wings on them. I think it's an elm . . . they are hooked on the tree. . . . It's home in

Excursion   *Comments*

a way. . . . Then they are blown free or let go—it seems impetuous—and go with the wind until they land. But the whole thing is rational, really; they are reproducing elms.

Leader: You mean that a seed pod doesn't seem to plan ahead . . . just takes off with the breeze, but down deep he knows: wherever I land I am going to grow into another elm tree?

In the Example step the Leader proves that he has listened and understood: while the Leader is a dedicated listener through the whole excursion, he must prove himself only in the Example step.

This serves some important purposes. First it gives the leader practice in understanding. Second, each completed exchange represents a transaction that is satisfying to both parties. The member has made a contribution, and it has been understood and appreciated. The leader has proved that he is able to foster communication.

Sam: Yeah, he's being sort of rational in spite of appearances.

Leader: Good! Any other Examples from nature of rational impetuousness?

Jim: How about an electric eel?

Excursion   *Comments*

Leader: OK. *(Looks at Jim expectantly.)*

Repeated transactions of this kind, where contribution and appreciation are the objectives, establish a tone, an intent, an atmosphere that speaks to a need we all have: to communicate with each other. This helps prepare group members and the leader for the demanding teamwork of Force Fit.

Jim: He generates this big charge of electricity . . . he must work to keep up to voltage all the time . . . and if anything touches him —wham!—they get it. That is impetuous but it is rational, too—it's a defense and a way of getting food.

Leader: I am intrigued by electric eel—maybe because I don't know much about it. Does anyone know about electric eels?

EXAMINATION

Harry: I know something about them.

Sam: So do I.

Leader: OK, let's examine electric eel. *(Writes: Examination: electric eel.)*

One of the criteria for selecting an Example for examination is that there be some knowledge in the group about

Excursion   *Comments*

it. If there is not, and the group is equipped with a simple encyclopedia, that may be used. The advantage of having an authority is that everyone in the group enjoys expanding his own knowledge. Any expert enjoys giving information. Also, this demonstrates that substantive knowledge on almost any bizarre subject can be valuable in this sort of meeting and encourages people to collect, as potentially useful, any bits of information that come their way.

Sam: Electric eels are found mostly in the northeastern rivers of South America. The amazing thing is that a six-footer has been metered at over 500 volts.

Harry: Another interesting thing is that the fishes or prey don't have to touch the eel. When he lets go, his head turns positive and his tail turns negative and the current flows between the two, all around the eel. It has to flow inside him, too, but apparently he is conductive.

Sam: The current . . . I mean the cells, or how he makes the current . . . these are

Excursion   *Comments*

litte disk-shaped things. **No** single one gives much voltage, but there are thousands of them.

Jim: That reminds me of an experiment I saw once where a guy used a sensitive potentiometer to prove that a lemon generates electricity.

Leader: Maybe every living thing does—but we have plenty of material here.

FORCE FIT

Leader: Let's go into Force Fit. *(Writes: Force Fit.)* How can we use this idea of an electric eel to help us solve our GAU? How make an ice tray disappear after ice is made?

Jim: Let's make the tray material sensitive to shock. When the ice is frozen and and you want some, you give the tray a shock and it disappears.

Leader: We have this magic material that is strong enough to hold the water but light enough or tender enough so that it can go up in smoke when . . .

This is not a complete idea, but may be the start of one. It is the leader's job to keep this idea alive until it is given more strength. If he can add to it, he does. If a member

Excursion   *Comments*

interrupts, the leader drops his own line of thought to pursue that of the member. The leader's primary job is to use the wits of his team.

Harry *(the expert):* Are you familiar with Cryovac? Well, it is heat-sensitive. It shrinks radically when heated. Could we make a disposable tray of Cryovac-like material?

Leader: How can we do that and not have to use hot water? Could we have it sensitive enough to shrink from your hand, and out comes the ice?

The leader watches the expert as members speculate. When the expert chooses something to explore, the leader gives him precedence because his depth of knowledge will permit him to see concrete possibilities. The only exception is that the leader does not allow the expert to be too critical too early.

Harry: What this suggests to me is something that would not be dependent on either hot water *or* your hand. We'll take this sensitive plastic, and we will make it sensitive to very low temperatures. We'll glue it to the tray and dividers with an elastic cement. When the water freezes, the temperature keeps going down. When it gets to, say, 20

Excursion	*Comments*
degrees, this film shrinks and leaves the ice cube loose.	
Leader: Harry, it sounds good. Now get tough about it: Can this work? Can you make a film like that?	
Harry: I don't really know, but it is an approach we have not thought of. If we *can* do it, we would like it.	When an idea is developed to the point where the expert is accepting it, the leader must force him to be critical. He thus takes from the expert the burden or blame for being negative.
Leader: OK, let's get it up as a Viewpoint. How shall I word it? (*Writes as dictated by the expert.*)	

PERSONAL-ANALOGY EXCURSION

This mechanism will be familiar to you, although the applications may seem strange. The following transcript includes all three mechanisms. The order is a useful one but not sacred. As you feel at home with the steps you should feel free to alter them in whatever way appeals to you. For example you might Force Fit right after Personal Analogy. Or when you develop your second set of Examples you might select one and ask for a Book Title.

PROBLEM AS GIVEN

(*Leader writes: PAG: How can we determine oil saturation in reservoir rock.*)

SYNECTICS FLOW CHART
PERSONAL-ANALOGY EXCURSION

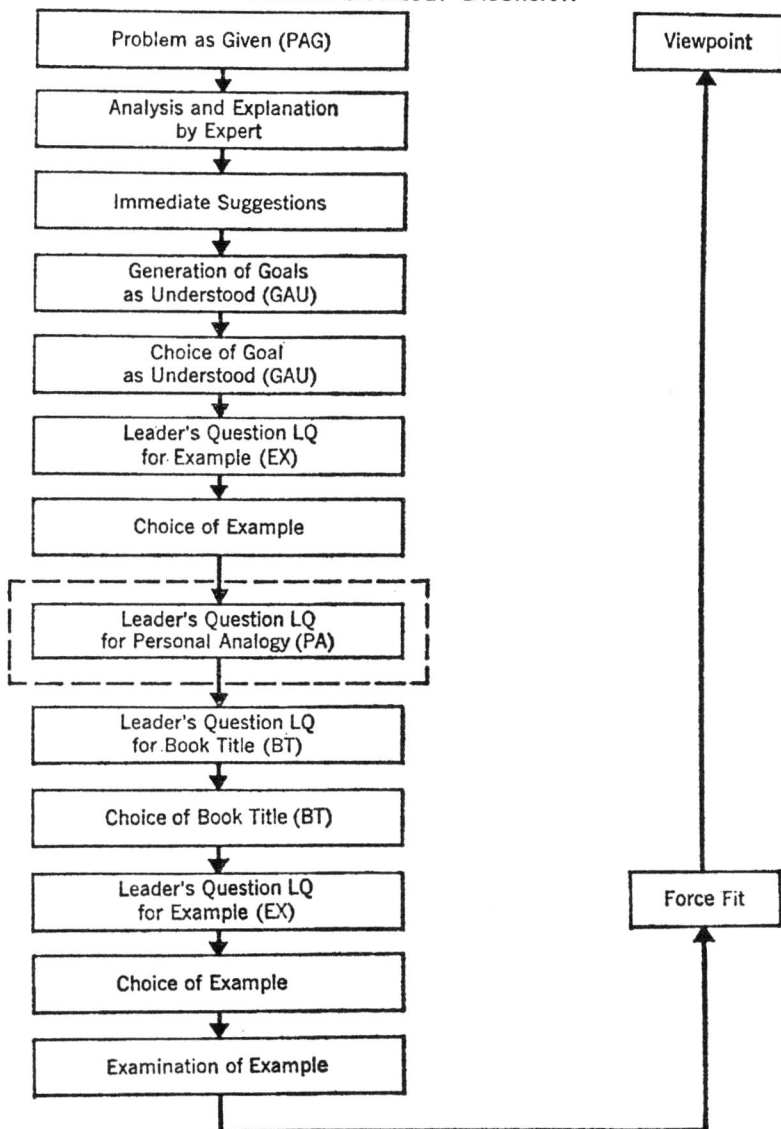

Comments

ANALYSIS

Expert: In the wells we are drilling now, it is a serious problem to get a sample rock that is an accurate representative of the reservoir. The best method so far is to put down a hollow bit (on the drill pipe) and cut a core. We bring up this sample of the reservoir rock and then try to guess how representative it is. The trouble is that we may have 3,000 pounds per square inch pressure at the reservoir. As we bring the core up through six or seven thousand feet of muddy water, this pressure is released. That and sloshing around in the muddy water make a big difference between the core we have in hand to examine and the reservoir. If we had accurate data on oil saturation, we could calculate the reserves and get better information on our recovery percentages— it would really do us a lot of good.

IMMEDIATE SUGGESTIONS

No solutions occur to the group.

Comments

GENERATION OF GOALS AS
UNDERSTOOD

1. How can I make reservoir rock tell me the truth?

2. How can I have oil tell me how crowded it is in the reservoir rock?

Excursion

CHOICE OF GAU

Leader: GAU number 2 has a lot of appeal. Let's go with that one. *(Writes: GAU #2.)*

LEADER'S QUESTION

Leader: My Question is for an Example from biology of a crowded situation. *(Writes: LQ:EX: From biology—example of crowded situation.)*

Toby: I don't mean it to be facetious, but flies on a cow flop.

Leader *(writes: Flies on a cow flop)*: Yes?

Toby: Well, it's a crowded situation. . . . I mean, those flies are two or three deep on there.

Excursion   *Comments*

Leader: It's such a rich source of food they really get in there and fight no matter what the crowd?

Toby: They sure do.

Bob: Anthill.

Kent: Virus culture.

Leader: Say more about virus culture.

The following Examples were given and listed as above. In each case the leader listened and gave feedback. However, we will, with one exception, simply list the Examples.

Kent: It is a funny kind of crowd. It might start out very thin, but it multiplies and makes itself a crowd.

Leader: Do you mean it is sort of dedicated to making a crowd of itself?

Kent: Partly that, but I was thinking that it has a deadly intention and needs a crowd to win.

Leader: OK—I think I get what you mean—killing is what its aim is, and the

Excursion *Comments*

bigger the crowd it makes,
the surer it can be of killing.

Kent: Exactly!

Toby: Womb with triplets.

Bob: Drop of sperm.

Kent: Seedling.

LEADER'S QUESTION FOR A
PERSONAL ANALOGY

Leader: Let's take this virus
culture. (*Writes: LQ:PA:
Virus culture.*)

Leader: Now, take thirty seconds—don't say anything
while you get into your
new skin—pretend you are
one virus in this culture.
How do you feel? (*Waits.*)

Bob: I am very small, but so
is everyone else. I am curled
like a corkscrew.

Leader writes as much as he
can.

Leader: Anyone feel different?

Leader shifts to different
member because Bob is being
very analytical. He is producing the sort of facts that the
Examination would produce.

Kent: It's nice and warm in
this culture, but I feel itchy.
. . . I am dissatisfied . . .

Excursion   *Comments*

because I want to go out
on my own . . . set up my
own culture. These guys are
too self-satisfied and smug
for me. . . . I'm going for   Leader writes key words and
a sensitive spot where I can   phrases. Asks speaker to slow
set up my own culture.   up if he is talking too fast.

Leader: Anybody have any   Leader wants as wide a vari-
other feelings?   ety as he can get.

Toby: I feel a sense of real
urgency . . . panic . . .
because I keep turning into
two of me and then four
. . . and everyone else is
doing it . . . I can feel the
food getting hard to get
. . . going to die . . . want
to do something fast but
nothing to do—except mul-
tiply. My only mission.

Leader: Your only mission?
Do you know who sent you
on your mission?

(Pause.)

Toby: Fate . . . no, not fate
really, it was evolution. I
wasn't always this way—
this prolific and deadly. I
have evolved . . . you
know . . . natural selection
—man, I have ancestors
who came over on the
Mayflower.

Excursion   *Comments*

Leader: Great! Does anyone feel differently about being a virus?

Bob: I hate the world. I want to get into some other place —out of this culture where I can kill other things alive. It's a black world . . . I want to murder.

Kent: I feel I am a very successful virus. With the way these other guys feel, I can sit back and relax, enjoy life and play a guitar. One is going to take care of reproducing and one killing. Why should I worry?

Toby: I resent his playing his guitar while I'm panicky.

LEADER'S QUESTION FOR A BOOK TITLE

Leader: This is a rich haul. Now my Question is for a Book Title. Can you give me a two-word title—poetic and compelling—that captures an essence of virus culture and contains a paradox? *(Writes: LQ:BT: For virus culture. (1) Essence (2) Paradox.)*

(Long Silence.)

Excursion   *Comments*

Leader: How about Kent's idea of warm and Bob's of murderous feelings. Can we make something of that?

Kent: How about Warm Hate?

Leader: The paradox is there, but I miss the essence. Tell me what you were thinking, will you? *(Writes: Warm Hate.)*

Kent: I just picked my warm and substituted hate for murder, but I guess a virus doesn't bother with hate.

Toby: Indifferent Destruction.

Leader *(writes: Indifferent Destruction.)*: You've got some of the essence—can we improve on "Indifferent" so the words fight more?

Toby: Also, how about Affectionate Destruction?

(Leader writes: Affectionate Destruction.)

Bob: Indifferent Purposefulness.

Leader *(writes it):* What are you thinking?

Excursion   *Comments*

Bob: From Toby's idea, the virus couldn't care less about his host, but he has a strong sense of purpose. Like Kent said in his PA—he's ambitious and wants to grow and multiply.

Kent: Compulsive Indifference.

Leader *(writes it):* Let's go with that.

LEADER'S QUESTION

Leader: My Question is for an Example from nature of compulsive indifference. *(Writes: LQ:EX: From nature—of compulsive indifference.)*

Kent: Queen bee.

Leader *(writes it):* Say more about this queen bee.

Kent: Well, I was thinking of their mating—she has the compulsion, but she flies away from males—higher and higher. When one of the males finally mates with her, she is indifferent enough to kill him.

Leader: Do you mean the way she plays hard to get—the

Excursion　　　　　　　　　　*Comments*

flying high even when she really wants sex, and then when she does let a male make it—killing him is a mixture of compulsion and indifference?

Kent: Yes.

Toby: Cat.

Leader: Yes?

Toby: A cat has compulsive curiosity, for instance, and yet the cats I know are quite indifferent to their owners.

Leader: If I get you, this is a strange combination in cats —being curious implies interest, even concern, yet a cat doesn't give a damn about her best friend—her owner.

Toby: Yes, they are a queer combination.

EXAMINATION

Leader: Let's examine cat. I've spent a lot of time wondering about them. (*Writes: Examination—cat.*) Anyone tell us more about cats?

While the leader does not specify anyone, he rests his eyes first on Toby, the originator of the cat idea.

Excursion   *Comments*

Toby: I've just been reading *Territorial Imperative* and so I'm biased, but it seems to me that each tomcat has a territory. He chases out the other toms and keeps the females for himself.

Bob: I think Toby is right. We had a big tom once, and he had a huge territory —several square blocks. He'd come stumbling home each morning with pieces chewed out of him. My five-year-old son, who owned him, said to him one morning, "Sniffer, is it worth it?"

Kent: You know the way cats lie perfectly still and relaxed? Every once in a while the tips of their tails flip as though to warn anyone, "I'm alert, baby!"

Toby: You know, a cat doesn't get surprised often. He really seems to know what's going on. He will be perfectly relaxed in your arms; you drop him and he falls on his feet.

Kent: A cat can be responsive, though; you pat or stroke him and gradually he relaxes and purrs.

Excursion   *Comments*

Bob: I think of cats as loners.
They don't travel around in
buddy packs like dogs.

FORCE FIT

Leader: Let's move into Force
Fit. (*Writes: Force Fit—
cat.*) How can we take this
idea of cat and use it to
help us have the oil tell us
how crowded it is in the
reservoir rock?

Kent: Something comes to
me. . . . If a cat gets
crowded, he loses all his
indifference . . . he gets into
a rage.

Leader: You mean we might
crowd the oil a little in
some way and then it
would yell and tell how
crowded . . .

Toby: I think I have a Viewpoint.

Leader: Are you going to
build on Kent's idea?

Toby: Well, no, it's different.

Leader: Please make a note,
and we'll come back to you.
Is there some way we can
put this oil in a rage so
it . . .

Excursion   *Comments*

Bob *(the expert):* If you take the pressure off, it becomes enraged. It boils and fumes and carries on. But you would like it . . . calm. You want to talk to it while it is not in a rage because then it is oil—like, it's got the essence of cat. . . . You don't want to talk to the cat when he is in a rage . . . he's not communicating.

Leader: How can we calm the oil down?

Kent: Stroke it!

Leader: OK, let's stroke it. What does it mean to stroke oil?

Kent: You stroke it just like a cat and it calms down, maybe it purrs. You stroke that oil.

Bob *(expert, musingly):* Yeah . . . you got to stroke it . . . stroke that oil.

Toby: It even arches its back as you stroke it—it will react to your stroking.

Bob *(softly):* Chill it . . . cool it down.

Leader: If you want, we'll freeze it. Pump liquid . . . what is that stuff?

Bob: Nitrogen! Maybe that's it. . . . We pump down nitrogen and freeze the hell out of that formation.

The leader has been watching Bob (the expert) closely. When he reacts, the leader goes with him.

Leader: We're with you. . . .

Bob: We'll freeze the water and the oil and everything and core right into it. Everything will stay right put.

Kent: Petrified candy.

Bob: We'll drill some and keep it cold some way. We freeze it and keep it cold as we bring it up. . . . We just might have something.

Leader: OK, there may be a few little details to work out, but let's get it up as a Viewpoint. How shall I word it? (*Writes as Bob dictates.*)

The general idea of freezing the core *in situ* so that all its character can be preserved was new to the expert and qualified as a Viewpoint.

7
Some Synectics Adventures

In a number of companies there are people who have taken Synectics courses and make use of the procedures when faced with a difficult problem. In some cases one person has an assigned responsibility to organize Synectics meetings for anyone who has an opportunity or problem. In other cases a whole department will be trained and will try to cooperate for more productive operations every day.

Kimberly-Clark, the company that makes Kleenex, recognized an opportunity area. They said to their Synectics group: the production side of facial tissue is very efficient; we have been reducing costs for years; see if you can invent some way to reduce the cost of distribution. After several meetings the group conceived the idea of pressing much of the air out of the tissues. More tissues could then be packed in the same size box, or the same number in a smaller box. This saved paperboard, shipping costs, and warehouse space. Nearly all Kleenex is now packed using the space-saving method.

In another case the manufacturer of counters, like those used in gasoline pumps to compute gallons and cost, wanted to increase the use of his product. A group used Synectics to develop the notion of a gasoline pump that would dispense a variety of octanes. Sunoco now uses this dial-your-own octane pump.

The records of the above meetings are long gone, but below are some more recent problems.

The transcript of a Synectics meeting fails to capture the overtones and sense of pleasure that occurs, but it may be revealing to you if I reconstruct briefly a few meetings. Although it is not indicated, the leader writes up on easel pads much of what is said. The following transcripts are condensed and edited. Actual meetings are far less pristine. In every case I have taken out the suggestions of immediate possible solutions.

SHORTAGE OF PSYCHIATRISTS

Problem as Given: How can we provide more diagnostic service with no more doctors?

Analysis: A large Boston hospital offers a twenty-four-hour diagnostic service for emotionally disturbed people. This clinic examines patients and prescribes a course of therapy. Patient load is increasing 50 percent a year but the number of doctors remains the same. How can the service be continued with no more doctors or money?

Goals as Understood:

1. How can one doctor be in three places at once?
2. How can patients be spaced throughout twenty-four hours?

Leader: Let's take number 1. In the world of nature, can you give me an example of being in three places at once? (*Note: In recommended procedure you would select an inorganic world because this is a people problem; however, this is obviously not critical.*)

Liz: Perfume.

Leader: Yes?

Liz: If you wear a distinctive perfume and go from one room to another you remain present in each room.

Leader: I think I see—you leave a trace of representation of yourself in each room?

Liz: Yes.

Dick: A fisherman's nets.

Leader: Go ahead.

Dick: I was thinking of a Japanese fisherman for some reason. He leaves one net in one place, another in another, and then collects them with the fish.

Leader: His nets act just as if he were there and catch the fish?

Dick: Yes.

Leader: Let's examine this fisherman's nets.

Dick: Japanese fishermen have to be efficient because they depend on a large catch to support their population. (*Note: Dick is more interested in the fish than the nets and his remarks lead the team down an unexpected path. The leader, noting their interest, happily goes with them.*)

Morris (*expert*): Some fish are considered great delicacies in Japan.

Peter: Yes, what is that poisonous fish that is so popular?

Morris: Poisonous?

Dick: I forget the name, but it has one poisonous part or a spot that has to be removed.

Liz: Who removes it? The person who eats it? I'd be nervous.

Dick: I am not sure, but it seems to me you remove it when you are eating it. In the article I saw it said that it is not unusual for people to get poisoned.

Peter: I would want to know all about that poison spot so I could protect myself.

Liz: You are right. I wouldn't trust the fisherman or the chef. I'd want to remove it myself.

Leader: OK, let's take these ideas about the fish. . . . How can we use them to put one doctor in three places at once?

(*Long silence.*)

Liz: There is something about do-it-yourself . . . get that poison out yourself.

Leader: Yes . . . this idea of protecting yourself? Can we help . . .

Peter: I don't know if it makes sense, but could the doctor use a patient as an assistant?

Morris (*expert*): We sure have plenty of patients and they have time to help—some have to wait for hours, which is another problem.

Dick: Could they help each other? Some kind of do-it-yourself group therapy while they are waiting to see the doctor?

Leader: You mean turn the waiting room into a floating group-therapy session?

Dick: Yes. *(To expert):* Could you?

Morris: I like the part about the patients getting some benefit while they wait—even if some just listened it would
probably be reassuring. But, I am a little concerned about
their working without supervision.

Liz: Could a nurse work with them, and perhaps get the
history of the next one to see the doctor or something?

Peter: Or could the patient just finished take the history of
the next one due to see the doctor?

Morris: If we push this thought to the end we have a floating
group-therapy session where everyone takes everyone
else's history. We would want a doctor there.

This was the Viewpoint. After experiments in the clinic
it has evolved to a free-form meeting in the waiting room.
One doctor presides. He and the group concentrate on
helping one patient plan his own course of therapy. The
doctor keeps an eye out for patients who are disturbed
by the openness. Anyone who prefers can have a private
interview. Most prefer the group treatment and find this
waiting-room experience rewarding.

THE CAR WHEELS LEAKED

Problem as Given: To quickly and inexpensively detect minute leaks in car wheels during final stages of production.

Analysis: A manufacturer of the steel car wheel upon which
tubeless tires fit had trouble with undetected "leakers."
Some were shipped with minute undetected holes and
used by new car manufacturers. Finished cars parked in
a holding area are only inches apart. When a "leaker" let
the tire go flat, the tilting car damaged the finish on itself
and the car next to it. The wheel manufacturer started
100 percent inspection, but it was further necessary to
power-spray the weld area of the wheels with dye and
inspect with black light. The "leakers" were detected,
but several cents cost was added.

Goals as Understood:

1. How can we make leakers identify themselves?
2. How can we prevent leakers in the first place?
3. How can we make leakers cure themselves?

Preventing leakers is clearly the most desirable solution of all and was not neglected, but this leader was influenced by the need for immediate action.

Leader: Let's take number 3 but put it aside for now and don't think of the problem. In the world of psychology think of an example of healing itself.

Ron: Forgetting.

Leader: Yes . . . would you say a little more?

Ron: I think forgetting a painful experience may be a healing of yourself.

Leader: If I understand, rather than continually being upset over something you forget it?

Ron: That's it.

Horace (the expert): A prejudice.

Leader: A prejudice, yes . . .

Horace: I think a prejudice is most often formed to allow a person to tolerate . . . or perhaps cope with a feeling, anxiety, or insecurity. I am not sure of that.

Leader: That doesn't matter. Are you saying that I have a feeling of discomfort with a black person—so to heal that unease I form a prejudice?

Horace: That's close to my meaning but you may have the anxiety and the prejudice without ever really being with a black person.

Leader: I see. Good. Let's take this prejudice idea. Take twenty seconds and I want you to turn yourself into a prejudice. Then tell me how it feels to be a prejudice. (Pause.) Yes, Dick? (Dick has given a signal that he is ready.)

Dick: I feel invincible and a little contempt for the person I am in. He never questioned my credentials, and in his hierarchy of prejudices I am just as important as his don't-jump-out-of-the-window prejudice. I've got it made.

Leader: Anyone have other feelings?

Al: I feel very grateful to my host because if he didn't nourish me and keep me, where would I be? I try to serve him and come to his mind often to keep that anxiety away.

Ron: I am ambitious, and once I am established I keep trying to grow. No matter what my owner does that bothers him I try to take credit. He squashes his finger in the car door and I say, "See, that black man on the way home put a hex on you."

Horace: I feel maligned by the way you guys talk—a person might think there were no good prejudices like me. I am for fair play and I have a constant fight for attention. I am put on red alert every time a hasty impulse comes along.

Leader: OK, let's take this material on prejudice and make some Book Titles—capture the essence but include a paradox.

Horace: Impulsive Care.

Ron: Anxious Contempt.

Horace: Insecure Invincibility.

Al: Malignant Gratefulness.

Leader: Good. Let's go to the world of modern tribal customs—can you give me an example of anxious contempt?

Dick: Speeding—we customarily break the speed laws and so we are showing contempt but there is nearly always, at least in me, a little anxiety about it.

Leader: Yes, I don't think anything of going 45 in a 25-mile-per-hour zone, but if I see a cop—even if he is looking the other way—I feel it strongly, so I am anxious all the time I am being contemptuous. Is that what you mean?

Dick: Yes.

Al: Cigarette smoking.

Leader: Yes, go ahead.

Al: I know it is bad, but I keep right on.

Leader: Do you mean that your actions show contempt, but in your mind you're anxious?

Al: Yes. It is stupid. We smoke because we are anxious, and it makes us anxious in another way when we smoke.

Leader: OK, let's examine speeding. What does this speeding idea bring to mind?

Ron: There is an exhilaration about speeding that is very sensual. It is, in a way, almost as exciting as sex.

Dick: Yes, even when you are not in control of it, like at take-off when they open up those engines.

Horace: I wonder if that is a male thing or do girls feel the same way?

Leader: What do you think, Horace?

Horace: It's probably in different degrees. I'm thinking of the difference in recklessness of girl drivers and boy drivers.

Al: I find that difference simply astonishing. Even young kids—say ten years old—girls have a different perception of consequences . . . they are more in the real world.

Horace: Right. But I think they turn suddenly unrealistic and into romantics at twenty-five.

Dick: I don't know about that. I believe women tend to be realistic most of the time.

Leader: Probably both can be true, but let's use this: Let's go back to our problem: How can we make leakers cure themselves? How can we use this speeding idea—any of them—to help us?

Al: I think of a cop speeding to the scene of . . . of a leak?

Leader: Yes, and then how can we . . .

Ron: He pulls his gun and fills the hole with lead.

Dick: The picture that came to my mind was he plugs it with his thumb like the little Dutch boy and the dike.

Leader: We could fill his gun with thumbs . . . but what is this saying?

Horace: I like the cop idea because we can do that—our dye speeds to the scene of the crime, but then it just lies there.

Ron: You know, on the side where you look for leaks with black light?

Horace: Yes.

Ron: Could you shoot lead or something wherever you see dye coming through?

Horace: You know, we have never thought of making a repair at that point. We were so obsessed with detecting we haven't thought of that. That is a good thought, but lead bothers me.

Leader: What concerns you, Horace?

Horace: These holes are really small—like pores, really. Black light shows you a stain, but that only tells the general area. We would have to have a very thin, dye-like lead that would stay molten until we knew it had filled the pore.

Al: Horace, could you use two different dyes—boy-girl type dyes? That turn thick?

Horace: Yes, I like the two components . . . like an epoxy. A slow curing one . . . But we have to make it really penetrate somehow.

Dick: I thought Al meant boy on one side, girl on the other.

Horace: That is it! A two-component epoxy, both thin as dye. Spray one on the outside, the other on the inside . . . they meet and react in the hole.

This Viewpoint was implemented on the production lines. It is fully automated and resulted in substantial savings.

SALLY NEEDED A JOB

The following is a one-man session held to solve a problem for a friend.

Problem as Given: Devise an interesting, profitable job for Sally B.

Analysis: Sally is a talented artist and writer who has been totally occupied with a family. The children are all away at school, and she wants some way to use her talents. She does not want to write copy or be a commercial artist.

Goals as Understood: How can she use good taste to make money?

Leader's Question: Book Title for taste: Anticipated Memory.

Leader's Question: From world of animals an example of anticipated memory. Answers: instinct, dog in heat, laughter, Pavlov's dog.

Leader's Question: Book Title for Pavlovian reaction. Answers: Rewardless Response, Empty Promise, True Mistake, Accurate Misinterpretation.

Leader's Question: From anywhere, an example of accurate misinterpretation: Answers: weather report, rhythm method of contraception, reaction to a come-hither look, woman and mirror.

Leader's Question: Examine weather report. The group makes many observations, many of them about history or past behavior of clouds, highs, lows, etc. In the end the meteorologist takes a guess and hopes nothing changes. There is comfort in "settling" the uncertainty.

Force Fit: Now how can we use this to help Sally? She is affected by the weather. Are people like weather? Are people interconnected with weather? Predict weather and predict moods? Does a person's history affect moods? Astrology says yes. How about a mood-predicting service? A mood-changing service is better. Sally's mood-changing service: person telephones Sally and answers questions about birth date, likes and dislikes (psychiatrist and psychologist design questionnaire). Computer has combination of personal interests and horoscope and specific local resources like museums, libraries, parks, etc. Whenever person feels blue he or she dials into computer, gets his horoscope for the day plus a suggested specific activity to change mood—for example, if the person is very sensitive to color and is eye-vectored, "Go to Boston Fine Arts Museum and study Rouault painting of clown on third floor."

The above session was held in 1965 before the present computerized horoscopes. In any case it provides a different though related service. Sally is painting and writing while she mulls over this suggested business.

NEW REWARD SYSTEM NEEDED

Problem as Given: Devise an effective incentive system for a research-and-development division.

Analysis: With modern technology so complex and new product development so many-faceted, rarely does any single person produce a new product. As an idea develops from concept to concept-testing to working model to prototype to market-testing to pilot production to test-marketing to production to full-scale marketing, there are many opportunities to help or hurt its chances of survival. Many people are involved. Since successful new products are so vital, how can we accurately assess and reward each person's contribution.

Goals as Understood:

1. How can we build helpfulness and new product support into present jobs?
2. How can we make a successful invention tell us who taught it how to succeed?
3. How can we centrally record and credit each erg of energy spent to help an idea?
4. How can we do the same for each erg spent to hurt an idea?
5. How can we give every helper a stake in success?
6. How can we make an invention accurately reward its fathers and mothers?

Leader: Let's work on number 5. Look at it hard for a moment and then put it out of your mind. Take this idea of stake—can you think of a Book Title for stake?

Ted *(the expert):* How about Risky Certainty?

Leader: Yes. What are you thinking of, Ted?

Ted: To have a stake in something means that it is certainly part yours, but whether the part will be worth anything is where the risk comes in.

Ralph: Rewarding Symbol.

Ted: Gambling Certainty.

Rachel: Wishful Reality.

Peter: Unrealized Reward.

John: Satisfying Ambiguity.

Leader: John, would you tell us what you are thinking with that?

John: The stake may be worth a lot or not worth anything, and that is ambiguous, but there is something satisfying about just having it.

Leader: I see. OK, now, in the world of chemistry can you think of an example of satisfying ambiguity?

Rachel: I think of a solvent.

Leader: Yes, a solvent. How are you thinking of it?

Rachel: What you are really interested in is the thing you are going to dissolve. The solvent is just a means, but it must feel rather powerful and satisfied.

Leader: Because it can simply take the solute all to pieces?

Rachel: Yes.

Ralph: A catalyst. No one knows its role, but it is very influential and powerful.

Leader: I think I see. . . . It's mysterious, but there is no doubt of its making things happen?

Ralph: Yes.

Leader: I see what you mean.

Ted: Water.

Leader: Yes. Will you say more about water?

Ted: Water is so common—so all over the place—we hardly notice it. It is background, but is involved in almost everything we do—nearly every reaction.

Leader: OK, let's go with water. Take a little time now and turn yourself into a little piece of water. Then I want to know how you feel.

John: Self-satisfied . . . I feel so pleased with myself I am embarrassed. I turn into vapor and get huge and keep admiring myself. This feels great. It's what I have always wanted to be.

Leader: Anyone feel differently?

Rachel: I am loving . . . so willing I will go along with anything. . . . I'm as embarrassed as John. If it wants to dissolve, I'll dissolve it. If it gets cold I'll freeze. I'm so willing I have no pride. No . . . I feel proud of being so willing.

Peter: I feel quite contrary, insidious and secretly powerful . . . even vicious. Like I will seep comfortingly into a tiny crack in a rock and then freeze and swell and burst the rock.

Ralph: I am important, so important that without me, not a wheel turns, not a seed grows, not a sparrow twitters. This must be how God feels.

Leader: This is something! OK, where were we? Oh. Let's go back to the problem. How give every helper a stake in success. How can we use this material on water to help us?

Ted: Everyone loves being water so much perhaps we should parcel out a lake or a piece of ocean among the helpers.

Leader: Do you mean actually give a "piece of water" as a reward?

Ted: I was really kidding, I guess.

Leader: There is something fascinating about the idea. Parceling out a lake . . . How can we use this?

John: You know, waterfront property is nearly unobtainable it is so desirable.

Ralph: The parceling idea is a winner, but who gets how much water or property? This idea of nothing happening without water—could every project start with thirty gallons of purple water? Every time the project manager needed something he pays for it with a pint or cup or even a gallon.

Peter: Yes and when the project succeeds I bring my half gallon of purple water and trade it for my half acre shore property.

Leader: Ted, is there something here, do you think?

Ted: Yes, there is—the idea of buying services this way is a new slant. Traditionally we think of the project budget as Ralph's thirty gallons. The project manager has a claim on Peter for a half gallon's worth. But the way we operate, Peter never sees a drop for his work for Ralph. He gets his cup a day from the company . . . reservoir.

Peter: The picture that comes to *my* mind is more eye dropper than cup.

Ted: Well, this instant stake for services—it is over and above the regular ration. It would be worth something or not depending on success. I just like that a lot. I do have a couple of concerns. An awful lot of people can be involved. The project manager in research can't know many in the marketing effort for example. How can he figure out who deserves what?

Rachel: Ted, let's use the way we budget a project: a few gallons to get through concept-testing—half to research and half to marketing. If we are still OK we get a lot more gallons—the project managers from research and marketing split the pool and so on down.

Ralph: So I am the package designer and I have a quart. I offer the artist a half pint and the market tester a half pint, and I keep the rest?

Rachel: Yes.

Leader: How about this, Ted? There are two ideas that I am hearing: one is you split up the thirty gallons into pools to get certain tasks accomplished; the other is that each pool is infinitely splitable, so that if a janitor caught a dropping test tube, the chemist might give him four pink drops instantly.

Ted: I like both of these, and I consider this a Viewpoint. Let's use certificates or percentages or something, because I can see Peter in his lab going into the pink-water bootleg business!

Peter: I won't dignify that, Ted; instead, here is the frosting for this beautiful cake: let every person involved make the distribution.

One version of the concept proposed that a pool be set up for each project. "Stock" certificates in it are printed, but the number of shares each certificate is worth is left blank. If *any* person makes a contribution, however small, to the project, he gets a certificate. As each phase of the project is completed, every person with a certificate is given a list of all other certificate holders in his area (research and development might be considered an area, marketing the other). He parcels out 100 percent to the people on his list according to his opinion of the contribution of each. For example, a technician who worked on the project believes his immediate boss hindered the project while the project manager helped it a lot. He gives his boss 0 percent and the project manager 20 percent, another technician 30 percent, and so on. He leaves himself off his own list. An impartial third party totals the percentages and adjusts them, and each participant gets a completed new certificate suitable for framing. A success-dependent amount of money is assigned to these "shares."

This proposal was in fact unacceptable to the company's president. The enthusiastic response of those in the company ·who would be getting the certificates (and making the new products successful) suggests that the president should have used the Spectrum Policy and let the group try to take care of his concerns.

POLARIS SUBMARINES HAVE GARBAGE PROBLEMS

Problem as Given: How get rid of garbage without giving away your position?

Analysis: A Polaris submarine goes to a station under the sea and remains there for as long as two months. Each day, the men aboard generate thirty cubic feet of garbage. This is presently (1959) disposed of in watertight bags weighted down with bricks. Approximately four thousand bricks are required per cruise. The navy wants to save that space and feels there must be a better way.

Goals as Understood:
1. How can we make garbage disappear?
2. How can we devise garbage that is heavier than water?
3. How can we avoid garbage completely?
4. How can we conceal garbage in the ocean?

Leader: Let's try number 4. Take the word "conceal." Can you think of a Book Title for "conceal"?

Tom: Well, it's furtive . . . how about Furtive Obviousness?

Sam: Hidden Obviousness.

Don: Unapparent Thereness.

Mac: Unobvious Distraction.

Reggie: Invisible Obviousness.

Leader: OK, let's move to an example. From the world of biology can you think of an example of Invisible Obviousness?

Don: Sex of a fish.

Leader: Yes?

Don: It is perfectly clear to a cod or a perch who the lady is, but it's invisible to me.

Leader: Do you mean that as a kind of outsider, things that are obvious to insiders are not to you?

Don: Yes.

Reggie: Antibodies. These become part of the blood, but they don't turn active or become apparent until the specific disease they are anti tries to attack. Then they rush to the scene and fight.

Leader: They are invisibly there until needed?

Ralph: Yes.

Leader: Let's take antibodies and examine it.

Reggie (the expert): Without them you'd die.

Tom: They are miraculous when you think of it. They police your body for trouble, and when they find it they take care of it.

Mac: Are you thinking of white corpuscles?

Leader: He may be, but it doesn't matter. Do you have something to add, Mac?

Mac: Well, the communication in the blood fascinates me. If we paid enough attention to signals, we would know within a minute or two when a flu bug strikes.

Leader: Fascinating! Let's take this material now. Our problem is to conceal garbage in the ocean. How can antibodies help us?

Sam: Let's add some antibodies to garbage that changes its refractive index so it's just like sea water.

Don: I can imagine grinding it up and encapsulating it to do that.

Leader: Can anyone help with this? We are turning it invisible, aren't we?

Tom: I can't help with refractive index, but since you have it ground up, let's encapsulate it with something heavy so it will sink.

Don: Use something tasty to fish.

Leader: We have a couple of things going here. Invisible, heavy, tasty. Reggie, will you respond to these?

Reggie (the expert): I am intrigued with all three; any one of them could solve the problem. The heavy and tasty would be easier, perhaps, than the invisible. I guess my concern is with the grinding and with the encapsulation. The garbage includes cans, glass, an occasional sneaker—you name it, and a lot of water.

Don: We can evaporate out the water—we can dehydrate the stuff. And maybe we can separate out the noisy glass and tin—they sink anyway.

Leader: That's right.

Mac: Let's use the glass and tin to weight down the lighter garbage.

Leader: Do you mean encapsulate in a sack, add light garbage, then heavy, until it is sinkable?

Mac: Yes.

Reggie: That will work. The segregating can be done, sharp corners taken off and everything, but we'll run out of the heavy stuff.

Sam: Could we somehow build in an antibody? Something that goes with the food and turns heavy when we want it to?

Don: Something that takes on weight when you want it to?

Sam: Yes, I'd like that.

Leader: Can anyone help us? Should we make this a new goal: How can we make garbage take on weight?

Tom: Take that communication idea—could we flow something through the ground-up garbage and deposit a weight on each tiny piece?

Leader: Use each piece as a "nucleation-site."

Don: Would the salt do that?

Leader: Sure. What do you want it to do?

Don: I am not sure but could we concentrate the sea water and make salt deposits on the pieces of garbage?

Reggie: Yes! We can get concentrated salt water from the evaporators and add that.

One of the proposals to the navy was to further concentrate the effluent from the evaporators (used to make fresh water from salt), make salt "bricks," and use them to weight down the garbage bags. What system the navy finally adopted is shrouded in secrecy.

HELP FOR A RELUCTANT DECISION MAKER

In this case a secretary to the president of a small firm had a problem. Her boss postponed decisions. Other people in the company, who needed his decision before they could act, badgered her for help. Carol, as we will call her, could not order her boss to do anything, but she believed that if a good, practical idea was developed she could persuade him to try it.

Problem as Given: How can we get Carol's boss to make decisions?

Goal as Understood: How can we make X an *eager* decision maker?

Leader's Question: From the world of *kitchen equipment*, an example of *eager*.

Example: Rotating spit.

Examination of rotating spit:

1. expensive current
2. same heat source and timer as control
3. different objects
4. active
5. cooks all at once, constant turning
6. regurgitating spit
7. self-basting
8. reappearing items temporarily out of sight
9. put on in certain order, take off in certain order
10. cooks more evenly, cooks more quickly
11. no cleaning

Get-Fired Force Fit

As explained previously, in the get-fired Force Fit each member is asked to select one of the pieces of examination and freely associate to it. He is to produce a deliberately *impractical* notion—one so absurd that if he suggested it to the boss he would be instantly fired.

Sharon: I picked self-basting.

Leader: Yes, OK.

Sharon: Everytime he makes a decision a little thing of confetti splashes all over him and messes up the office—distracts him—and there are little horns that blow and dancing girls.

Leader: OK, good. That should get you fired. Sally?

Sally: Rotating—have him do the rotating—have him in sort of a wheel thing and he has to reach out and grab a stationary decision and then he's stuck with it and he turns around until he makes it.

Leader: That will do it. Jerry?

Jerry: Regurgitating the spit.

Leader: Yes.

Jerry: Have it set up so there's a little electric control on his chair and whenever he picks up a thing if he puts it down without making a decision it'll make him— It will shock him.

Leader: Very good. Peter?

Peter: Have all these decisions in different objects—have them all hung up all over the room in beautiful containers. He walks through them.

Leader: Yes.

Peter: As he walks through them he kicks or breaks them or whatever.

Leader: OK, yes. Carol?

Carol: Somebody stole my idea. Can I go back to my original beautiful thought in this whole thing—reappearing item —which is sort of an electronic-type switchboard that sort of flashes.

Leader: Is this something you already suggested to the group?

Sharon: I think you thought of that before you came.

Leader: Let's not use new material to reinvent something you already have.

Carol: OK.

Leader: Just pick one—cooks all at once. What comes to your mind? What does "cooks all at once" make you think?

Carol: Simultaneous.

Leader: Yes, simultaneous. What else do you think? Just talk about what comes to your mind.

Carol: Ten minutes a day he has to sit there and have twenty people stand there and simultaneously throw things at him. Each one has to have an answer.

Leader: Yes, good. All right, now, everybody's fired. Let's go back and see if we can get you your job back. Sharon, you had self-basting. Whenever he makes a decision confetti goes flying around and horns blow and dancing girls come whistling through. How can we make this really work? What does this suggest that we really do.

Sharon: Reward him.

Leader: Yes, give him some marvelous reward. What does he love more than anything that we could give him for each decision?

Sharon: Peace.

Leader: Peace. Does that mean the party goes on until he makes a decision and then there's a lovely quiet for about two minutes?

Jerry: It's like hitting yourself on the head and stopping. It would be noisy until he decided, and then he would be rewarded with silence for two minutes.

Leader: How can we make this happen in some practical way?

Jerry: What if a— The picture that comes to my mind is that there is a gradually increasing tension or sound. Somehow it is focused at him. If he doesn't make a decision about something it keeps getting louder and louder, and when he makes a decision it shuts off for about five minutes and then it starts to build up again until he makes another decision.

Sally: You could have cuckoo clocks.

Jerry: Like—

Leader: Like what?

(Jerry draws a head popping out of a wall.)

Sally: That's really what I had in mind.

Leader: You pop in about every twenty-five minutes and say, "Have you made a decision?" Is there any way we can use this sort of suggestion here?

Peter: Well, isn't there some sort of reward in developing a good decision?

Leader: Yes. Is there any way— How can we— Can this be projected to him? It would be great to make decisions and instantly get the reward of knowing it's right.

Peter: Earlier we talked about his getting opinions before making decisions. Now this says reverse it. Do it the other way. Make the decision and *then* get opinions.

Leader: Wonderful. This would give him a little delay time —peace for a while, too.

Sally: Oh, I like that. He says, "This is what I've decided." Then Carol takes it to other people for their opinions.

It is just a temporary decision, and he can change it if the opinions are too strong.

Leader: This sounds interesting. It flies in the face of what a "good" manager is supposed to do, but it has a beautiful, antihypocritical ring. . . . Carol, what do you think?

Carol: I think the idea of making decisions twice . . . well, it is tough enough once and—

Leader: I hear what you are saying. You are having trouble listening to the idea because it goes against—

Carol: I can't tell you what I like about it because I am very involved. I would hate the thought of getting the decision and then having to get that decision over again.

Leader: I know, Carol. You really can't bear to consider all the consequences that you see in this idea. But suppose for a minute that by seeming to make the decision less final you actually make it twenty times as easy for him to make it? Do you see what the implication is? Then it will only take a minute. He says, "Well, I want to do this. This is my temporary decision. I'll do this and then I'll see what feedback I get." It's done and out of the way. When it comes back it's two-thirds made. Particularly if the opinions support it. So dealing with it twice may take only a twentieth of the time as dealing with it once. Now this is a very strange notion that's come up here. In other words it's making him make a decision twice instead of once. It's making it tentative the first time to get some feedback, so it's an entirely new way so far as I know of looking at and making a decision.

Sally: It might also put off the psychological thing or whatever it was about it in the first place that he didn't want to tackle.

Jerry: Exactly. It lets him make a decision without really making it. "This does not count. I'll try it on for size." That may be his whole hang-up, for all we know.

Peter: But it nonetheless needs to be rewarding; consequently, some portion of the decision is made. Am I reading this right? In other words, in a way he is saying all right for this part of it or all right provided we chase it down or somebody else chases it down.

Jerry: Well, the mechanism, it seems to me, has a built-in reward. If this guy has trouble making decisions, apparently there's something about it that hurts him, and it's probably the imagined pain of being wrong. What we're doing is removing some of the pain by having him make it in little bits that aren't really . . . that don't count until he really says they do. The beauty of this, it seems to me, is that he can make a pretend decision. It has no consequences. Then, Carol, you go and get the panel he's selected, the panel of people he would have respect for, and you say, "Quick give me your opinion," and when it comes back to him for his final decision the hard part is perhaps over for him. I don't know.

Carol: Now I can like it, I think. I was going to say it's also good because at that point you do know it's on his mind. As it is, you don't really know whether he's even read something and knows he has to make a decision. He's giving it more thought and coming to a much more definite idea of what he wants to do, so that's very good from that point of view.

Leader: OK. What shall we put down? I know you have some concerns about it and you think, "My God, twice the exposure, it may take twice as long." This is a speculation. This is an invention, and you don't know it will work until you try it. And of course you'd have to get his OK about it. How should we put this down?

Carol: OK. Alleviate traumas of decision making.

Leader: What's the mechanism of actually carrying it out?

Carol: Initial action: get people, a panel of people that he approves of. We might have two or three panels—a, b, and c—which represent different areas. Maybe one is money expertise, another design expertise, and so on. X makes his initial decision and marks it "panel a and c." I take it to them and they give their opinions. I bring their opinions back, and X says, "OK, that's final," or he changes it.

A NEW TOOTHBRUSHING SYSTEM

The following session was run by a company in England. The general purpose was to develop new teeth-cleaning products that would appeal to children. The children themselves found the experience one they like to repeat. The meeting continued and produced a concept that the company is testing. The material leading to the idea and the idea itself have been deleted at their request.

Participants: Jamie, six; Bridget, eight; Peter, five and a half; Tony, seven and a half; Janet, six.

Problem as Given: How can we make children clean their teeth regularly?

Janet: Tell them.

Leader: What? Get mummies and daddies to tell them? Is everyone sure what they've got to do, or do you want to ask some questions? Now, then, let's just talk about cleaning teeth so that everyone knows what everyone else does.

Tony: Put toothpaste on a toothbrush.

Leader: Out of a tube?

Tony: Yes.

Leader: Do you have a special toothbrush, that's smaller than mummy's and daddy's, or do you have one that's the same size?

Jamie: Smaller.

Leader: Everyone has the same, do they?

Group: Yes.

Leader: Let's do something else now. If you can write, write it down; if you can't, it doesn't matter, just remember it and tell it to me later. If you can, think about the problem and put down how you understand it, what you think the problem is. If you can, put another sentence in place of the Problem as Given: "How to do something." What do you think makes children want to clean their teeth?

Bridget: The nice flavor that the toothpaste has.

Leader: How to make toothpaste have a nice flavor, then? That's another way of solving the problem, isn't it? What else is there about a toothpaste that makes you want to use it?

Jamie: I don't like it at all; it stings.

Leader: Shall we say, "How to make a toothpaste that doesn't sting"?

Jamie: Yes!

Leader: Let's look at it from another point of view. Why do you actually use the toothpaste?

Bridget: Because if you don't it will make your teeth bad.

Leader: In other words, you want to make your teeth strong and healthy. How can we put that in a sentence? How to do something. How to tell children they need strong and healthy teeth.

Bridget: Yes. If you don't use toothpaste your teeth may become bad and have to be taken out and you'll have to have false teeth.

Leader: How to stop losing your teeth and getting false ones. Has anyone been to the dentist yet?

Tony: Yes.

Leader: Did you like it? Did *you?* Oh, everyone likes going to the dentist, do they?

Group: Yes.

Leader: Can that help us in any way?

Peter: Yes.

Leader: So if I put down "How to make children go to the dentist regularly"—is that all right?

Peter: Yes.

Leader: What we've got to do now is forget about the problem. Let's take "strong and healthy." I want you to try and think of things that are strong and healthy in buildings.

Jamie: The walls.

Leader: Why are they strong and healthy?

Jamie: They're put together strongly.

Leader: I see. You're saying they're put together strongly with concrete and cement. I see—that's one example. Peter's got one.

Peter: The chairs.

Leader: Can you tell us about the chair, then, Peter?

Peter: They're clean.

Leader: So that means they're healthy.

Peter: And they're strong because they're fixed together with screws and nails.

Leader: They have to be strong, otherwise when you sat on them they'd fall to bits, wouldn't they?

Peter: Yes.

Leader: Right. That was another example. What was your example, Janet? You had your hand up. You've forgotten; think again, then. See if you can think of any more examples of strong and healthy things in buildings. Jamie's got another one.

Jamie: Doors.

Leader: Why are doors strong and healthy?

Jamie: Because they're fixed to the wall with hinges.

Leader: So these hinges make the door strong.

Peter: The pipes.

Leader: The pipes?

Peter: They're strong because they're fixed to the wall by clips.

Leader: Why are they healthy? . . . If it's your waste pipe it takes all the dirty water away, doesn't it? So that makes them very healthy, doesn't it? They're strong as you say because they're fixed to the wall with clips.

Tony: Floor boards.

Leader: How are they strong and healthy?

Tony: Because if you stood on them and they weren't strong you'd just fall through.

Leader: How are they healthy? Can you think of it? I think I can. See if you can.

Bridget: They keep out the dirt from the earth.

Leader: If you didn't have them you'd be walking on a dirt floor, wouldn't you? Let's take one of these; let's take the wall, or a wall. Pretend you're a wall, and tell me how you feel to be a wall.

Peter: It's all solid and hard.

Leader: You feel solid and hard, do you?

Bridget: You get hit by balls when people are playing ball.

Leader: How does that feel then?

Bridget: Bumpy.

Leader: You feel bumped, then.

Tony: People climb over you.

Leader: How do you feel?

Tony: Horrible!

Leader: How does anyone else feel?

Jamie: When somebody opens the doors.

Leader: How does that feel then?

Jamie: Hurt.

Tony: Bored.

Leader: Why do you feel bored?

Tony: Because I have to stand there all the time.

Peter: I've got light switches and things fixed to me.

Leader: How does that feel?

Peter: I've got screws sticking in me.

Leader: Yes, so how do you think it feels, Peter, to have a screw sticking in you?

Peter: Hurt.

Leader: You're feeling hurt as well, are you? So I'll put "hurt" again and "Screws sticking in you." Everyone's saying they're feeling horrible and hurt and bored. Does anyone feel anything different to that—on the happy side? Do you, Jamie? How about you, Janet? Would you feel happy if you were a wall—no? Nobody feels happy at all. It's a miserable life, is it?

(Silence.)

Leader: Can we think of examples of things that stay there all the time in . . . family life?

Peter: At night you stay in the house all the time.

Jamie: The house.

Leader: It would be a bit nasty if the house walked away while you were asleep, wouldn't it?

(Laughter.)

Bridget: The clock.

Tony: It doesn't always have the same time.

Leader: Does it always stay at the same time?

Group: No.

Leader: Never mind, it always stays where you've got it, doesn't it?

Janet: Telephone.

Tony: Yes, telephone.

Janet: Television.

Tony: Ours goes into the kitchen sometimes.

Leader: It's always in the home, isn't it? It doesn't go away.

Peter: A light switch.

Leader: You like light switches, don't you? That stays there because it's stuck in the wall, doesn't it, with screws that hurt you?

Jamie: Door handle.

Leader: You're all talking about the house. What about the people?

Peter: Arms.

Leader: You mean these arms? They're always on you, aren't they?

Tony: A whole body.

Leader: What do you mean?

Tony: Well, you're always there.

Janet: Doors.

Leader: Let's take the door handle. I want you to be a door handle. Let's have a good think about it. You've all thought of something, have you? Let's start with Jamie.

Jamie: People open the door, then they turn the door handle.

Leader: How does this make you feel, then?

Jamie: It feels as if they're twisting me.

Tony: It feels horrible.

Tony: You'd have screws in you 'cause you're screwed to the door, so you wouldn't fall off.

Leader: How does that make you feel?

Tony: Quite happy.

Leader: How does everyone else feel? What would happen if you weren't there?

Peter: The door wouldn't open.

Leader: So how does that make you feel, being the handle of the door?

Tony: Proud.

Leader: Why are you proud?

Tony: Because you're in charge of the door.

Peter: Because I stay around all the time.

Leader: Now we've got lots of things here that are opposite. Somebody feels happy, somebody feels horrible, somebody feels proud, and somebody feels bored. What I want you to try and do is to sum up all these opposites in two words that describe the door handle. I'll give you an example straight from here. If we link those two words together, we get "horrible proud." Now when you're proud, you don't normally feel horrible, do you? They're opposites, but they describe the door handle. Can anyone think of things like this—for the door han-

dle? It doesn't matter if it's not very good because somebody might be able to help you.

Tony: Happily Bored.

Leader: Tell us why a door handle is happily bored.

Bridget: He's happy because he doesn't fall off the door and
he's bored because he has to stay there all the time.

Leader: Now, any more?

Peter: You're happy but you're proud. You're proud because
you're in charge of the door, and you're happy because
you don't fall off of it.

Leader: Can we make that into two words, what Peter said?

Jamie: Horribly Happy.

Leader: Can you think of anything? You don't have to use
these words. Keep imagining you're the door handle, and
how a door handle feels and what it looks like and what
it does.

Peter: It goes straight and then it comes out rounded.

Leader: So it's straight and it's rounded. Can somebody get
that into two words?

Tony: Straightly Rounded.

Leader: Now that sounds peculiar, doesn't it?

Group: Yes.

Leader: How can something be straight and round? Well a
door handle is, isn't it?

Bridget: Longly thin.

Leader: All right then, good! Now can you think of examples of something in Nature that is Horribly Happy?

Bridget: Dandelions. They're happy because they grow, but
they're horrible.

Leader: Yes, they're a weed. They're not very welcome, and
they don't look very nice either. But they're happy because they're growing there.

Jamie: Trees.

Tony: Because people climb them.

Leader: Hang on a minute, Tony. Let Jamie tell us first.

Jamie: It's horrible because it's brown and black.

Leader: But why is a tree happy?

Jamie: Because it has flowers and leaves and things.

Leader: That's very good. Were you going to say the same
thing, Tony?

Tony: Yes.

Bridget: Thistles. They are happy to be growing, but they're horribly prickly.

Leader: Yes, fine. Shall we talk about dandelions for a while? Tell me what you know about dandelions.

Tony: They have lots and lots of little yellow things sticking out:

Leader: Anything else we know about them?

Bridget: They're green and yellow; they've got green leaves and yellow petals.

Leader: Do you know anything else?

Jamie: They're weeds.

Peter: They've got prickly leaves.

Group: They haven't.

Leader: That doesn't matter. Peter thinks they have, and that's all that matters.

Tony: People say if you pick them you go to the toilet.

Leader: That's interesting. What does anybody else know about dandelions?

Tony: At first people call them dandelion clocks.

Leader: Why are they called dandelion clocks, then?

Jamie: Because they've got little silvery-gray things and, you see, when you blow them, they come out, and you count how many times you blow them. That is the time, the number o'clock.

Leader: What are these silver-gray things, then?

Tony: A sort of fluff.

Bridget: They're seeds.

Leader: What else? What happens to their seeds?

Tony: Well, they blow away and then they grow more.

Leader: Any more? *(Silence.)* No?

Now, then, comes the difficult bit. Now we've got to solve the problem. Can you remember what it was? Here you are: "How to make children clean their teeth regularly." Is there anything in here? I'll read it out to you. We're going to use this to see if we can solve the problem. I'll read it out.

Lots and lots of little yellow things.

Green leaves and yellow petals.

They're weeds.

They've got prickly leaves.

People say if you pick them you go to the toilet.

People call them dandelion clocks.

They've got little silvery-gray things. When you blow them, they come out, and you count how many times you blow them. That is the time, the number o'clock.

They blow away and then they grow more.

Can you see anything there that will help us solve the problem?

Bridget: No.

Leader: This is where everybody helps everybody else.

Jamie: When you look at the time, when it's evening and when it's morning, and sometimes when it's the afternoon, you look at the time and you know it's time to clean your teeth.

Leader: I see. So Jamie's saying that we get something that at the right time tells us to clean our teeth.

Jamie: Yes.

Leader: How can we do this? Can anybody help Jamie there?

Peter: You could use the dandelion flowers in helping to make the toothpaste.

Leader: I see. Let's think about it. We've got the dandelion as a clock, can we use this at all? Can't anyone think how we can use the dandelion in a clock, or people think it's a clock?

Bridget: You could use the juice in the stem to make the toothpaste.

Leader: We might be able to, but how about using the clock bit to help tell children that it's time to clean their teeth? Have you got clocks at home? But do you use the clock? Do you look at the clock and think it's time to clean your teeth?

Group: No.

Leader: Could we get the clock to tell *you* it was time to clean your teeth?

Tony: Have an alarm.

Bridget: Tell them the time and give them a dandelion clock. Blow on a dandelion clock and tell them what the time is, and tell them that that time is the time that they should clean their teeth.

Tony: But we haven't got a dandelion clock.

Leader: Well, couldn't we make one? Couldn't we use one of those clocks that are used to teach you to tell the time? One that doesn't tick around, one that somebody moves the hands around?

Peter: We've got one at school.

Leader: Couldn't we make one with dandelions?

Bridget: Yes.

Peter: If you turn the hands to the right time, it would stay at the right time till you turned the hands again.

Leader: How are we going to use this to tell the children it's time to clean their teeth? Come on, I need your help, I can't solve the problem, so I want you to do my work for me, I hope, if you solve the problem. Can the fact that they're weeds help us at all? *(Silence.)* Nothing? How about yellow things sticking out of the green leaves. Is there anything there? Don't forget that we're trying to make children clean their teeth regularly.

Bridget: They might have yellow things sticking out of their teeth if they don't clean them regularly.

Leader: I see. We've got to tell the children about this somehow, haven't we?

Tony: The mums and dads could tell them.

Leader: Yes. So in fact what we do is tell the mums and dads to tell them. But what do we tell the mums and dads to tell them? There are times when your dad tells you to wash your face—you don't do it, do you? Like all children you're naughty sometimes. We've got to make them want to clean their teeth.

Tony: Well, make a toothpaste with a special taste.

Leader: Can we call this special taste—dandelion? Would this help?

Tony: They would buy it if we gave something free away, then they would go and buy it.

Leader: Would they? Doesn't Mummy go and buy the toothpaste? Do you go with her? You see what you want and you tell her, do you? Do you, Jamie? Do you, Janet? Do you?

Group: Yes.

Leader: So it's not Mummy who buys the toothpaste; it's
    you do, really?

Tony: Mummy *buys* it.

Leader: Mummy pays the money, but you tell her what to
    get. I see. So that if there was a nice toothpaste there,
    this would help, would it?

Tony: You could give something away with it as well.

Leader: What could we give away that would be . . .

Peter: Couldn't you make it free?

Leader: Well, we couldn't do that, could we?

Bridget: We could give away packets of sweets.

Leader: Well, what do sweets do to your teeth?

Tony: Make them bad.

Leader: But we could give away special sweets that don't
    do anything to your teeth. In fact, sweets that help
    clean your teeth. Do you think this would make chil-
    dren clean their teeth more regularly?

Bridget: Yes.

Tony: I expect they would use it up to get some more.

Peter: To get some more of the sweets.

Leader: We'll put this up as an idea, shall we?

Leader: We had another idea, didn't we, about the dandelion
    clock? Is there anything here that we could give away
    free with the toothpaste?

Jamie: You could give a dandelion away with it.

Leader: We'd have to give them a plastic dandelion, wouldn't
    we? We couldn't give a proper one. Would you buy
    it with a plastic dandelion?

Tony: No.

Jamie: Yes. We could put a little bit of string on it, you have
    a face and you put two hands on it and you have a big
    key.

Leader: Yes, I see it. You can give something away free that
    you can make a clock out of. Can everybody see that?
    You know, with one tube you could give away the
    hands of a clock, with another tube something else.

  I see, we give away parts of a dandelion clock. You can
    have the times at which you should clean your teeth
    on it, couldn't you?

Bridget: Make the toothbrush one of the hands of the clock.

Leader: That's an idea, so when it gets to the right time you know you've got to use it.

Jamie: You could get a stalk and then some bristles, fix them onto the stalk, and you would make a toothbrush.

Leader: Like a do-it-yourself toothbrush kit. Can that last sentence help us? Blow away and grow more dandelions.

Bridget: When the toothbrush of the dandelion falls to pieces, they could get another dandelion and make another one.

8

The Uses of Creativity

The practice of creativity must begin with yourself. You obtain the greatest leverage by investing time and thought in making more and better use of the talent you now own. The first step is to become even more sensitive to the problems that surround you. Each problem is an opportunity to exercise, develop, and test your skill. Tackle each one you see—privately at first. In each case you first collect more extensive data within yourself. These include facts, opinions, feelings, and even seemingly irrelevant material. Second you use these data as a launching pad for loose speculating. You use your wit and energy to search out and pursue the possibly useful rather than pick out and concentrate on flaws. Only in season do you give formal recognition to shortcomings, and even then they are identified as something to be overcome.

This mode of behavior can be profitably applied in a wide variety of situations. It can be rewarding as you work alone, but eventually your greatest return will come in meetings when you are working with one or more other people.

Because the second rewarding area in which to practice creativity is in the use of others, there is an expression "He uses other people." The sense is "He exploits other people." I mean use in a different sense: you invite others to make their contribution. You know the result will be different if the others contribute, and you want that difference.

The third general way to practice creativity for more satisfaction is in discovering and using actuality. All around us are traditional, accepted practices that only *seem* sensible and efficient because we have thought of no alternatives. If we consciously make a practice of creativity, we are better able to see and change the absurdities that surround us.

How can you practice creativity to use yourself, others, and actuality better? Synectics procedures—listening, supporting the good in a weak idea, using an analogy to renew speculation, taking a vacation from a problem—were familiar to you before you read this book. But by gathering together these tenuously connected, occasional behaviors and showing that they are the sinews of creativity, we hoped to show that creativity is something you already have. In this chapter we will indicate some areas of opportunity for practice. Most of these opportunities declare themselves as discomforts. Whenever you feel frustration, boredom, anxiety, anger, or helplessness, it is a signal. Instead of suffering through it, look for the problem and go to work on it. When you fail to use your creative problem-solving talent, you strike at the quality of your own life. The problem will appear impossible for you to solve. That is why you feel frustrated, bored, or incapable. Even though you feel helpless, find some small subproblem you can cope with as a beginning.

For example, Jane, a saleslady in a large department store, could not get along with her supervisor, Mrs. Blum. The other salesladies also had difficulties with Mrs. Blum, who was very critical and quick to lose her temper. Jane began to treat this as a problem she could solve. Some immediate suggestions that occurred to her were firing the supervisor or getting rid of her in some more violent fashion. Just using the Spectrum on the idea of firing Mrs. Blum made Jane feel better about the problem. She decided that even if she could fire the supervisor (which was not actually a possibility), she would not do it. She would first give the supervisor a warning to treat her salesladies more thoughtfully. Jane then turned this into a Goal: How to make the supervisor always treat Jane thoughtfully.

For a few days Jane observed the supervisor. She noticed that Mrs. Blum often became angry when Jane or any other saleslady asked a question such as, "What should I do about this dirty blouse?" Jane experimented. She asked no questions of Mrs. Blum. When she needed information she asked other salesladies. This was not successful. Mrs. Blum was still angrily critical of Jane. Jane's next experiment was to make up her own mind about what to do about a problem. For instance, she found a slightly damaged shirt and decided it probably should be sent to the basement as a second. She then took the shirt to Mrs. Blum and said, "I believe this shirt should go to the basement as a second. Should I take it there?" Mrs. Blum examined it and said, "Yes, but make out a transfer slip to give us credit." This experiment was successful. Jane began to make up her own answers to questions and simply check them with Mrs. Blum. It changed their relationship. Mrs. Blum was much less critical of Jane and seldom showed anger or impatience with her.

In this culture, like any other, the establishment conspires to make each of us a compliant member. Cooperative behavior is often rewarded with material plenty. This is a beguiling reward. Who does not want plenty? So most of us are co-conspirators. Too few of us realize that there is a whole spectrum of alternatives. If we have the power to understand that a problem exists we have a worthwhile start. For example, it is quite feasible to have a life of plenty *and* of satisfying quality, too. Each of us deserves no less.

John Holt has written extensively about the use and effect of fear in education.[1] It seems to me that wherever we find fear of authority we should look for the thoughtless establishment. This may bring us close to home.

[1] John Holt, *How Children Fail.*

Also there is little doubt that education is one of the best designed, most pervasive, most effective servants of the status quo. In conversation John Holt has said, "Any kid who is not paranoid by the time he graduates from high school is crazy." He went on to point out that each child, by mastering language, has demonstrated the astonishing power, range, and subtlety of his intellect before he gets to school. Instead of continuing to flower and flourish the child is systematically taught his limitations.

Almost no one wants to let his talents lie idle. There is a whole body of myths that are built up to support the establishment; including such well-thumbed nodders as: If a man has a guaranteed income, he won't work; The janitor really gets a kick out of his job—he doesn't want any more responsibility; Most people are lazy. Anyone can prove, with examples, that these statements are true. It is like breaking a man's legs and saying he can't walk. But most high school dropouts and graduates take jobs that use a fraction of their capabilities. So do most college graduates. An efficiency expert will work and scheme for days to fully utilize an expensive machine tool. But the man who operates it or the woman who types or the middle manager is given superficial courses, and is under-utilized. Management *is* concerned, but there is little agreement on what to do. Creative behavior here can pay vast dividends. The first step is to be aware of problems. The next is to tackle one—then another and another. Make use of yourself. Enlist and use others to help you. The best way to produce change is to invent an alternative that everyone prefers to the existing mode.

This illuminates a heart-lifting phenomenon. When you use yourself better and learn to depend on your capabilities, you will do the same with others. It then follows that you will be more able to use actuality. Thus the three uses of creativity are self-reinforcing. Indeed many of the problems that confront you exist because at some time someone failed to use actuality. For example, the president of a large corporation and his four group vice presidents had employed a consultant to study ways they could cut costs in distribution for their twelve decentralized divisions. The recommendation indicated that the company could make worthwhile savings by using a central computer to control inventory. The division managers were sent copies of the report and advised that computer control would be initiated as soon as practicable. Every general manager responded instantly with a carefully reasoned explanation of why computer control would seriously handicap his division. Those twelve angry letters were the signal that the president and group vice presidents had failed to use actuality, and as a result all seventeen men were ingeniously working at cross-purposes. The president's office belatedly practiced creativity and used the actuality of their position. The appropriate vice president wrote each general manager, "Your letter makes it clear that there are serious shortcomings in the proposed system. It will not be installed until you and we have together overcome these difficulties." And the whole group met to develop a means of achieving the savings without the disadvantages. The meeting was exhilarating for everyone involved. Each person's concerns were treated as Goals as Understood—something to be worked toward. The final system was better and more satisfying than anything a consultant could have designed.

We are surrounded by evidence of the power for accomplishment that is fostered by democracy and free enterprise. I believe our corporations are so successful because the people who make them so ignore, whenever possible, the authoritarian structure, which somehow goes against the grain. Our own inclination to respect the individual more than the structure is sounder than our rational acceptance of the superior-inferior, parent-child relationship. But imagination makes authoritarians of us all: if I treat my subordinate as an equal, if I welcome his ideas and thoughts and use them, won't he take over my job? Won't my boss wonder about my value? Won't my child get out of hand?

These fears are fostered by our competitive culture. Our deep Pavlovian response to someone else's good work is dismay: I am losing. This keeps our view of actuality slightly out of focus. Rationally I know that when my subordinates do well it is good for me, too. But emotionally I react differently. This confusion makes it difficult for managers to see and act with clarity. Judgment is not a manager's most important function. As we have said, a manager is in actuality, before anything else, a teacher. He uses his skill in seeing and solving problems not to solve them and hand down edicts but to teach how to spot problems and how to codevelop alternatives with those involved.

Furthermore, competition is so deeply respected and has such healthy connotations (where would the human race be without it?) that I hesitate to question its usefulness. But there is no question that in group problem solving, competition, in the usual sense, is destructive. I suspect that on a larger scale, competition for favor, respect, and advancement in a company is just as wasteful and destructive. But how will we select the fittest? It is a problem we are concerned with now, and I am certain it will be solved because some fine thinkers are imagining possible solutions.[2] But to be able to take full advantage of the ideas of others requires creative behavior.

Education, learning, and changing are so closely related to problem solving that they may all be names for the same thing. We are taught bad habits in our present system. Our view of life gets warped, misty, and softened by what happens to us as we are brought up, educated, employed, and retired. A young child knows precisely what his mission in life is. It is to learn, change, and grow: to

[2] See Jay W. Forrester, "A New Corporate Design," and Warren G. Bennis, *Changing Organizations* (New York: McGraw-Hill Book Company, Inc., 1966).

accomplish. It appears to be an exhilarating, rewarding mission.[3] I believe that the over-all mission never changes. It continues to be: learn, change, grow so you can accomplish. The three uses of creativity serve this mission.

A child is a good model to pattern yourself after. He sees his life as a series of problems or serious games. From learning to use his hands, to climbing on the table to get the lamp, he goes about his problem solving with inventive relish. You should consciously do the same. Your problems may be more complex, with many ramifications, like how to deal with an authoritarian, negative boss. But this is what you have been in training for since birth. Problem solving is the single activity you are precisely designed to do. Problem solving is not peripheral to life, it is what living is.

Many who participate in Synectics training go back home and adapt parts of the procedures to work and family life. Psychologists, businessmen, architects, housewives, scientists, teachers, and ministers have found many of these concepts as valuable in their fields as have inventors. This is not surprising. Inventing, improvising, solving—each of us should be aware that these are everyday activities.

Obviously Synectics does not offer a panacea; it is clear to you by now that there is no magic in the procedures. The magic comes from people. Good listening and the Spectrum Policy can be valuable anywhere. An executive from the Midwest recently told us over the telephone, "I said to my son [thirteen], 'You know, I have not been listening to you and you have not been listening to me. From now on we are going to play a game—even when we are angry.' We have been playing listen and feedback ever since. I am really getting an education!"

Peter Drucker, of the Graduate School of Business at NYU, discussed the results of his study of research man-

[3] See George P. Leonard, *Education and Ecstasy*.

agement. "Contrary to what Wall Street analysts seem to believe," he says, "there seems to be almost no correlation between research budget and research results . . . very rarely is there a real difference in the quality of the people who do the research between the companies that get their research money back a thousand-fold and those that have nothing to show for all their time, money and efforts." He went on to explain that what *does* determine the success of an innovating activity, whether in research or marketing, is "top management, and especially the chief executive officer. It is not what he does that matters so much. *It is primarily his attitude.*" (Italics mine.) "The chief executive who . . . forces himself into the right positive attitude towards ideas for the new and different will create, throughout his organization, the attitude and the receptivity that makes innovation possible."[4]

Remember that your attitudes are perceived through behaviors that are substantially under your control and can be modified. When an influential executive makes it his habit to behave in a constructively demanding way he sets a style that can be consciously imitated by others: the consequences are far-reaching. The same applies to opposite behavior.

We have encountered a number of executives who have this constructive style, and we have questioned their subordinates. Such a man is viewed as:

A risk taker who absorbs the risks taken by those who work for him—a man or woman who relieves his subordinates of the burden of failure for ideas that don't work out.

A man who can live with half-conceived, half-developed ideas and not insist on considering only finished products.

A man who is willing to find ways to get around company procedures that impede achievement.

A man who has a fast take-off time, who is willing to take action with an idea that looks good even when complete data are not available.

[4] Peter Drucker, *SBANE Bulletin*, April 1967.

A man who is a skillful and constructive listener.

A man who doesn't dwell on mistakes—either his own or others'.

A man who relishes what he is up to.

There are also many such men and women who are not executives but ministers, housewives, appliance repairmen, and warehousemen. The characteristic they all share is a confidence, a respect, an appreciation of individuals—beginning with oneself. Life is a finite problem or series of problems that he, by using himself and those around him, can understand and solve. In many ways the atmosphere induced by such a person is creative. As Drucker mentioned, it is an *attitude* that is important here, and the value of that attitude is not restricted to a Synectics problem-solving meeting. For instance, the value and pleasure of a traditional business meeting or a cocktail party conversation is greatly increased by the presence of one such individual. I recently had dinner with the general manager of a company and several of the people who work for him. The conversation was about a philosophy of life, what sort of principles were most important. It was lively and there were very different points of view, but I became aware of an unusual feeling of well-being among the group, a glow that came from something other than drink. As I watched the exchanges I believe I saw the source of satisfaction. Many observations were directed to the general manager. His attention to each speaker was complete. His responses were open and candid and each started with a statement like, "You know, you are absolutely right in..." and he would refer to some part of the speaker's view. He might go on to voice a contrary view, but he had first firmly established his respect for the speaker. This man was unfamiliar with Synectics but had learned to use the most important element of it: appreciation of others.

We are working with people in community projects,

church affairs, and education as well as with businessmen and women. Synectics procedures, because they are based on use of every individual, help representatives of opposed groups work out their differences. By asking each person to develop a wishful goal as he understands the problem, it becomes possible for people in conflict to work together. For example in a labor-management contract dispute a labor member's goal could be: How can we bring the pressure of a strike on management without leaving our jobs? A manager might wish: How can we prove our determination without shutting down the plant? This suggests a combination that both could work on: How can we bring to bear strike pressures without the drawbacks? This may seem an absurd goal but our experience tells us it can be reached. This creative behavior helps people to work their way beyond vested positions, away from debate, and toward cooperation. In a strange way, conflict is a signal that people have an opportunity together. Handled creatively, both can win. Handled carelessly, both will lose.

The deliberate use of metaphor provides a common language for people of different backgrounds. A teen-ager can think of an example of conflict in the world of weather that is just as interesting and useful as a mature scientist's example. The metaphorical approach makes it clear that *any* individual's way of seeing the world is valuable. A Synectics Excursion on one level might be thought of as a way of mentally shaking hands and establishing an intent to cooperate.

Every individual is helpful to a Synectics problem-solving session. The appreciation of an individual's metaphor leads to seeing that each individual is useful, and this helps overcome stereotyping and prejudice. Carl Rogers says that to enter this type of relationship with another person takes courage because it opens up the possibility of a change in yourself, and such a change in attitude implies that you were wrong: this is both difficult and painful.

In Synectics meetings the primary goal is to identify and solve a problem. Being wrong has no stigma; indeed a wrong idea is often used to start toward a useful Viewpoint. Everyone slips into wrong behaviors now and then: a reminder is appropriate, expected, and without heat. Since all the participants, even the old hands, are having the same experience, this camaraderie in change is a help and a comfort.

As for the type of problem or opportunity for which Synectics can be helpful, we suspect there are few limits. My own bias is that when a decision depends upon the selection between two or more *known* alternatives, Synectics will be least useful—for instance, when a company is deciding whether to make or buy an ingredient for one of its products. Some devotees say, "You should avoid purely evaluative situations like that. You should ask, 'How can I get the advantages of making (or buying) without the disadvantages?'"

We observe that too often meetings are held to make a decision when too few alternatives have been developed. The obvious penalty is settling for less than the best alternative. We also find that using Synectics helps problem solvers remain flexible. You don't feel that you must choose between alternatives A, Y, and P. You pick part of A, part of Y, and a modification of P and discover a fresh alternative. A less obvious penalty of too few alternatives is that because those concerned have not worked hard on the problem, they have failed to understand it. For example, a company group was working on the problem of increasing the sale of their floor tile. Management believed that the problem would 'be solved by a new product with demonstrable advantage. As the group worked, collecting information, developing goals and Viewpoints, and testing them wherever possible, two areas of opportunity emerged that had little to do with the product itself. First, it was discovered that existing distribution channels were aimed toward industry and institutions (appropriate for their other company products but not for consumer floor tile). A family found it very difficult to find this product, let alone buy it. Second, the group learned that housewives decided color and design. They have trouble making this choice and are bothered by feelings of uncertainty. The group then invented a simple viewing device that permits the housewife to see how her own rooms will actually look with a given floor tile. These two opportunities suggested a third: a salesman equipped with viewer and samples could do a better job in the home than a traditional salesman in a store. The group developed a modified house-to-house selling concept that was responsive to both the buyers' needs and the company's lack of distribution.

The conscious practice of creativity as an everyday activity is particularly valuable because it permits you to rationalize, accept, and gradually *expect* miracles of yourself.

Appendix 1

GLOSSARY

Analysis: The explanation by the expert of the Problem as Given.

Book Title (BT): A two-word phrase that captures the essence and paradox of a particular thing or set of feelings. This is usually a combination of an adjective and a noun.

Examination (EXAM): Factual and associatory material generated about the subject under discussion.

Example (EX): A direct comparison of parallel facts, knowledge, or technology.

Excursion: The development of metaphorical material during a Synectics meeting.

Force Fit (FF): The use of the seemingly irrelevant metaphorical material to generate possible new approaches to the problem.

Goal as Understood (GAU): A restatement of the problem as seen by each individual or a statement of a goal a member believes would be desirable.

Immediate Suggestions: Immediate solutions offered by group members.

Leader's Question (LQ): A question that requires an analogical or metaphorical response.

People Problem: When the problem or opportunity has to do with people—their actions and feelings—rather than with a mechanism or thing. In this type of problem possible solutions are more diffuse, less clear cut and provable. Force Fit is more demanding. An example of a People Problem is: How to get congress to pass a minimum income law.

Personal Analogy (PA): An empathic identification with an object.

Possible Solution: A possible new approach to a problem. It is not a solution until it has been made to work.

Problem as Given (PAG): A brief statement of the problem.

The Spectrum Policy: A way of viewing an idea. At first, look for the positive aspects of a new idea before verbalizing the negative points.

Thing Problem: Has as its objective the development of a device or system. An example of a Thing Problem is: Devise a more efficient process to desalinate sea water.

Appendix 2

New-Product Problems—Hardware-Oriented

Devise a more efficient fuel cell.

Invent an easier way of applying paint.

Devise an instant, portable radio antenna thirty feet tall that travels in a small package.

Devise a profitable use for a waste by-product.

Expand an interesting piece of technology into a commercial product line.

Conceive of a new home appliance that fulfills a need that no one is now aware of.

In one model of an army personnel carrier, land mines tend to trigger a gasoline explosion in the fuel tanks. How can this be prevented without major alteration?

Process Problems—Business-Oriented

Devise a continuing education program in a company— one that will keep employees interested and alert and will avoid obsolescence.

Conceive of a more effective method for acidizing oil-bearing limestone strata.

How can we inexpensively add one pound of chemical to two tons of grain and have each grain get its fair share?

Devise a new market strategy for a dying brand.

How can a manager in a technical area be most helpful when a subordinate has a technical problem?

Devise a system for presenting ideas that gives them a maximum possibility for constructive consideration.

Devise an idea-incentive system that will encourage involvement on the part of everyone from janitor to vice president.

Process Problems—People-Oriented

How can a bored clergyman renew himself?

How can we make the visiting-physician program in Vietnam produce more lasting benefits for Vietnamese physicians?

How can an individual reduce his prejudices?   ·

Conceive of the physical facilities of a new architectural school that satisfies the needs of the interested parties (students, faculty, townspeople, etc.).

Devise an economical system in which both a slow and a fast student can be given what each needs in the same class.

How can we persuade those in power in the _____ church to pass this power downward in an orderly fashion?

Conceive a meaningful way to involve people in the democratic process from childhood on.

Appendix 3

INTERVENING WITHOUT MANIPULATING

The leader who encourages each individual of the group to give his own unique response to the various questions he asks (Example, Personal Analogy, Force Fit, etc.) will make the best use of his group. In both Synectics and more traditional meetings the leader must handle each person with care even if it seems clear the person is attempting to put down another. Below are some so-called intraverbals, phrases that encourage a direction without imposing or narrowing. These are intended as specific examples of how to express an intent. You are welcome to use them but also make up your own that feel comfortable to you.

OK.
What you want to do, if I get you, is . . .
Good, yes?
Do you have an idea how to do that?
What would you like it to be? *(looking for information)*
Great.
How about that? What is your feeling about that? *(direct to expert)*
Any other thoughts about this?
I'd like you to word it . . .
What about that? *(to expert)*
What is particularly useful about . . . ?
What is your concern about this?
Can we draw something out of this?
What is appealing about that?
Would you write a goal based on that? *(slight change in subject)*

This is very useful.

I am not sure. Let me hear. *(bring out bashful ideas)*

Let's wish for the real thing.

Good. Great. The more difference the better.

Wait a minute. *(slow speaker down)*

What is your reaction?

Let's put that one down. *(new goal)*

That is the kind of solution I like because . . .

Very interesting.

Say more about it. *(draw out idea)*

Anybody feel different? *(personal analogy)*

What comes to your mind?

I want just anything at all that comes to your mind. *(examine)*

It's fine. *(reassurance)*

Is there some way we could use this so that . . . ? *(overcome objection)*

You have an idea. How might we do that?

What would you like it to be?

Can we improve on this?

Write it down. *(when someone interrupts with new idea)*

How should I word this? *(to expert)*

Tell me more.

What do you like about this?

What's on your mind?

Tell us about it—we don't care.

Is there some way we could use this? *(and turn it around)*

Keep talking.

I love the idea that . . . but can we add to that by . . . ?

How can we use this idea?

That's an interesting notion, what do you think?

Why don't you put the meanings to the words that you like.

How about that?

What specifically is implied there that you like? What concerns you about it?

Could you phrase that as a goal?

I'd like you to word it in such a way that it directs us to do something.

What would make this more effective?

Can you give me some words? *(in writing a goal or possible solution)*

I think I've got you. How can we put that? *(discourages person from monopolizing the conversation)*

Can we go on?

Can we do any more with this? If not, shall we make it into a goal?

Anything goes here.

I have the feeling that here is a marvelous goal. If no one has a solution, I'd like to put it up.

How can we turn that into a goal and keep all the pluses?

Rather than raise a philosophical question, can you word it as a goal so we can do something about it?

What are you thinking?

What is your reaction?

Any others?

Have you got it written down?

What is bothering you?

What you said is very desirable.

If I get you what you want to do is . . . *(making sure you understand)*

This notion is very valuable because . . .

Sounds as if it might be a possible solution.

Can you wish for something?

Would you like to address a goal to a bigger problem?

Maybe we can build on that.

Appendix 4

SUGGESTIONS FOR NEW USES
AND NEED FINDING

The dilemma in these problems or opportunities is that one does not know what he is looking for. The most effective procedure we have found is to search for Goals as Understood. These can then be attacked in the usual way.

There are three approaches we have often found rewarding.

1. You are a _____.

   If you are looking for opportunities in, say, the kitchen, your LQ might be, "You are the kitchen. How do you feel?" A variation that is sometimes rewarding is, "You are a *hostile* kitchen. How do you feel?"

2. Characteristics of this person _____.

   You personalize either the product or the area (bar of soap or kitchen) and list character traits. Look them over for a Book Title and proceed to an Excursion.

3. Examination of _____.

   Carry out an examination of the product or area as you would examine an Example. It is useful to be speculative. Then go on to develop a Book Title and proceed with the Excursion.

Appendix 5

MUSEUM EXPERIMENT

We used this experiment in courses to help people learn to see that most man-made things are the result of solving a problem. It is rewarding to look at objects in this way because it puts them in context and reinforces both wonder and the contemplation of possibilities.

Visit a museum. Go to the sections that exhibit the artifacts of ancient cultures (Eskimo, Polynesian, American Indian, African, etc.). Examine these useful tools and objects.

Pick out one of these artifacts that particularly appeals to you as an elegant invention in its day. Study it in detail and speculate upon the way it might have been invented.

After leaving the museum write, by yourself, the scenario of an imagined Synectics session that took place long ago when the artifact you chose was invented. Make up the PAG it solved. Try a couple of immediate suggestions and answer them as expert. Formulate a GAU and then the complete Excursion that ends triumphantly inventing the artifact. Enjoy yourself, take any liberties you like, but include (even if not articulated) all the steps of Synectics. Try to lose yourself in your EX, PA, BT, EX, EXAM, and Excursion. Use only the worlds that would have been available to the time period you choose.

Appendix 6

WORLDS

This list of worlds to search in for Examples is meant only to suggest possibilities. Feel free to create your own worlds—for example, world of paint brushes, world of firewood, etc.

ORGANIC

Biology
Tribal customs
Sports
Fashion
Dancing
War
History
Mythology
Botany
Philosophy
Theater
Education
Animals
Politics
Racing
Espionage
Comedy
Art
Movies
Criminology
Witchcraft
Exploration

Archaeology
Medicine
Science fiction
Computers
Models
Agriculture
Time and space
Noise
Acoustics
Finance

INORGANIC

Physics
Mineralogy
Woodworking
Chemistry
Mathematics
Electricity
Astronomy
Machines
Rocks
Metalworking
Oceanography
Geology
Architecture
Meteorology
Bridges
Aeronautics
Astrophysics
Buildings
Transportation
Synthetics

Bibliography

Alexander, Tom. "The Wild Birds Find a Corporate Roost." *Fortune*, August 1964.

Beveridge, W. I. B. *The Art of Scientific Investigation*. New York: Random House, 1957.

Blake, R. R., and Mouton, J. S. *The Managerial Grid*. Houston: Gulf Publishing Company, 1964.

Bradford, Leland P., Gibb, J. R., and Benne, K. D. *T-Group Theory and Laboratory Method*. New York: John Wiley & Sons, 1964.

Drucker, P. F. "Marketing—How to Make It Productive." *New England Business*, vol. 18, no. 4 (April 1967).

Engelmann, Siegfried and Therese. *Give Your Child a Superior Mind*. New York: Simon and Schuster, 1966.

Forrester, Jay W. "A New Corporate Design." *Industrial Management Review*, vol. 7, no. 1 (Fall 1965).

———. "The Glass Revolution." *Newsweek*, Nov. 23, 1964.

Hilgard, Ernest R. *The Experience of Hypnosis*. New York: Harcourt, Brace & World, 1968.

Holt, John. *How Children Fail*. New York: Dell Publishing Company, 1964.

Jay, Antony. *Management and Machiavelli*. New York: Holt, Rinehart and Winston, 1968.

Kepner, C. H., and Tregoe, B. B. *The Rational Manager*. New York: McGraw-Hill Book Company, 1965.

Kubie, Lawrence S. *Neurotic Distortion of the Creative Process*. New York: Noonday Press, 1956.

Leonard, George P. *Education and Ecstasy*. New York: Delacorte Press, 1968.

Papenek, V. J. "Solving Problems Creatively." *Manage-

ment Views, vol. 9, pt. 3. Selected speeches from the academic year 1963–1964.

Parnes, S. J. *Creative Behavior Guidebook.* New York: Charles Scribner's Sons, 1967.

Rogers, Carl R. "Communication: Its Blocking and Its Facilitation." *Northwestern University Information,* vol. 20, no. 25 (April 22, 1962).

Schutz, William C. *Joy: Expanding Human Awareness.* New York: Grove Press, 1967.

Index

Index

expert and, 67
in ice-tray problem, 139–140
in oil-well problem, 157
in people problem, 108
search for, 221
in thermos-bottle-closure problem, 129, 131
wishful thinking and, 120, 129
Gordon, W. J. J., ix–xi

Habits, changing, 86
Holt, John, 203
Humor, 58, 61
in Force Fit, 104–105
Hypnosis, 81
Hypothesis formation, 10

Ice-tray problem, 66–71
Book Title Excursion, 138–154
Ideas
development of, 77–79
encouragement of, 24–25, 32, 39
expert's attitude toward, 67–71
incubation (mulling over), 77–78, 83–84
nondestructive response to, 58–61
putting aside, 61
in Spectrum Policy, 46–52, 59
Imaginative speculation, see Speculation
Incentive system, problem, 177–181
Inspiration, 83–84, 98–99
Intervention without manipulation, 217–219

Jay, Anton, quoted, 1
Job seeker, problem, 176–177
Jung, Carl Gustav, 81

Kepner, Charles H., 15
Kimberly-Clark Company, 169
Koestler, Arthur, 80
Kubie, Lawrence, quoted, 86–87

Leader
expert and, 64
frustration and boredom of, 63
and Goal as Understood, 92–93
ideas suggested by, 57
intervention without manipulation, list of phrases, 217–219
as listener, 58
manipulation avoided, 62–64
meeting model for, 37–41
need for, 55–56
nondestructive response to ideas, 58–61
role of, 6–8, 55–65
rotation of, 6, 64
and Synectics terminology, 116–117
Leader's Question (LQ), 94–95
in automobile safety session, 121–123
in ice-tray problem, 140, 143–144
in oil-well problem, 157, 159, 163
in people problem, 109
in thermos-bottle-closure problem, 131
Listening, 28–29, 41–46, 207
by leader, 58

Manager, function, 2
Manipulation, 62–65
intervention without, 217–219

Discovering Discounting/Revenge:
the First Law of Social Interaction

The following article was among George Prince's unpublished writings after his death.

I still remember the first time I noticed what I've come to call the "First Law of Social Interaction." We were working with a new group of five men and one woman. They were working on a new loss-proof closure for the Thermos. We made it a practice to tape group processes and I was outside watching the action on television. Soon after they got under way, I stepped out briefly to get a snack. When I got back, the group was discussing who would do what. "Jim" offered to "hold the crayon" and was readily accepted by the group. Then he turned to "Sally" and said, "Since you are the only woman in the group, why don't you keep the notes?" (At the time, this was a culturally acceptable assumption to make.)

The group began to offer ideas or raise questions and learn more about the problem. Jim was a good leader and also a good participant, and the ideas flowed. At one point, Jim joined the idea givers. He picked up the Thermos and passed his hand over the opening. "We take a sheet of plastic and... "

"That would be too expensive," said Sally. Jim and the group bought Sally's objection and continued thinking of ways to solve the problem. They developed several approaches in the remaining time. Then they broke for refreshments and to review the tape. As the tape ran back, I noticed what I had missed during my snack: Jim singling out Sally to keep the notes. Now her negative comment made sense, as it connected to her earlier feeling of discount. I asked her if she remembered Jim's telling her to be secretary of the group. She most definitely did, but she didn't remember what she was thinking when Jim offered the sheet of plastic idea. That marked the beginning of my fascination with discounts.

Discount/Revenge

"Our survival and development depend on our capacity to recruit the invested attention of others to us."
       - Robert Kegan, author of *The Evolving Self*

A discount is any action, body language or verbal behavior that I perceive as a put-down, criticism, or denigration. Revenge is defensive, though it may appear as aggression. It is payback for a discount. It may involve openly discounting the person who injured me, subverting that person's goals or attempts at organization, being uncooperative, open rebellion or quietly going "on strike" by emotionally withdrawing from a common enterprise, or any other form of retribution. Discount/Revenge is an integral part of the Validation Deficit Syndrome. Whenever I am devalidated, the Discount/Revenge cycle is triggered. All my other agendas are put on hold, and I search for a strategy to recoup and put it into effect as soon as possible. If immediate action is not feasible, I wait for a better time to get revenge. I do not forget. I have had the experience of feeling discounted and resolving not to get revenge. At a later time when an opportunity for revenge occurs, I strike without conscious thought.

This compulsion to retaliate bears examination because it is a major destructive force in nearly all our lives. As noted, I first observed it in the Jim and Sally incident, but have since seen it in action countless times. The videotapes made it plainly clear. Initially I considered retaliation childish. Why would a mature person waste energy on such a useless activity? After seeing it happen again and again and again and again, without ever encountering a "mature person," I revised my thinking. Invalidation begets revenge in almost everyone, including those would are emotionally mature. Discount/Revenge is a reliable behavioral law. It might be for behavior the equivalent of the law of gravity for the physical world: a basic fact that must be accounted for if you wish to navigate truly successfully in social interactions.

The Impact of Discounting

Once aware of this phenomenon I began to use videotape review as well as direct observation to keep track of its various forms and their effect on the target person in invention groups. True to other natural laws, it became clear that a discount aimed at a specific person had an impact not only on the target person, but on all who observed it. The higher the status of the discounter, the greater the increase in defensiveness in the group. Thousands of observations confirmed the concrete actions that affect the field and thus influence participants toward collaboration or building toward competition and strife.

The simple social phenomenon of discount and revenge can have far-reaching consequences. The effect on relationships is profound. From the growth and development of a child or an adult, to the nourishment of the connection-making capacity of group members, to the availability of participants in a group to work together constructively—all can be devastated. Discounting can create a hidden dynamic in any organization, one that impairs group efficiency and undermines the organization's goals because it fosters non-cooperation and worse.

If developmental behavior were a concrete substance, then the smallest component of developmental matter would be what we could call a behavioral sub-atomic particle. In the language of quantum physics, discounts and validations are two different kinds of invisible waves that create fields that bring out very different behaviors. The Discount field tends to evoke the disintegrating forces of agitation and entropy; Validation invites harmony and synergy. When I present these actions in these black and white terms it oversimplifies. Many of the actions that trigger disorder have valuable contributions to make, for example, pointing out flaws, or insisting on precision, or raising questions. This is why these actions are so widely tolerated. They are like chemotherapy to a cancer patient—the side effects are devastating and he suffers them in the hope that the beneficial effects will outweigh the damage. But clearly they need to be done carefully and thoughtfully to get the possible benefits without the toxic side effects.

The only counter to discounting is validation, but even validation does not erase the consequences of discounting. To the degree that validating experiences outweigh those of discounting, I dare to stay available to interact with others. My feelings of worth give me the courage to risk interchange. I have something of value to offer. But the two experiences are separate and immiscible, like oil and water. I retain the scars of discounting. Validation is a way to nourish my intrinsic drive to constructive growth. Validating actions are those that encourage responsibility, appreciate competence and risk-taking, and that demonstrate love and inclusion. If as a child, I experienced a great deal of validation and little or no discounting, I will usually develop relating skills that recruit others into positive relationships. People will be drawn to me since validation begets validation. Those who have not had that experience need to be treated with extra care and attention.

Though the rule of discount/validation applies to everyone at all times. Any time we disagree with someone— whether a co-worker, a rival, or someone we love— whether we're in a specially focused group meeting or any place else, it is important and helpful to be sensitive to how we present dissenting views. We should focus on the positive aspects of someone else's ideas. And if they disagree with us, we should be prepared to feel slighted when someone else disagrees with us. That feeling hurt is natural, but we don't have to react negatively to it. How we react is an option. Some itches are better left unscratched.

Unrecognized Discounts

Below is a sample collection of everyday phrases that seem harmless, yet we have observed that when they are used, the person addressed reacts as though discounted.

That seems to make sense, but...
Better than that...
I've heard that before.
To be serious ...
No, no. Absolutely not.
 Let me challenge that.
I disagree with you.
Let me see if I can pin you down on that.
The trouble with that is ...
Wrong.
Not where I come from.
I have a problem with that.
I question that.
Let me play devil' s advocate.
Not to contradict you, but...
I don't want to insult your intelligence, but...
I don't know about that.
What makes you think that is true?
I happen to know something about this.
That is against my principles.
That is ridiculous.
Get your facts straight.
Where did you get that idea?
Let me tell you how it is done.
What John means ...
Let me ask you a question.

Building on *The Practice of Creativity* Through Synecticsworld

Synecticsworld helps organizations develop their own creativity to solve even very complex problems. They do this through a range of approaches designed to support collaborative cultures committed to teamwork while eliciting the creative power of each participant.

Synecticsworld works in three key areas: creating and activating growth strategies of your business or nonprofit as a whole, developing specific product and marketing strategies, and improving the work culture and performance of your organization.

Cofounded by George Prince, Synecticsworld has over 50 years of experience working with teams on the building of successful innovation.

If you wish to learn more about Synectics or benefit from a seminar for you, your organization or a product or service launch, go to:
www.Synecticsworld.com

Synecticsworld has six locations on three continents.
Their main office in the United States is at:
29 Elm Street
Cambridge, MA 02139
(617) 868-6530

For Further Reading

• *The Art of Innovation: Lessons in Creativity from IDEO, America's Leading Design Firm* by Tom Kelley, Jonathan Littman and Tom Peters

• *Business Model Generation: A Handbook for Visionaries, Game Changers, and Challengers* by Alexander Osterwalder and Yves Pigneur

• *Change by Design: How Design Thinking Transforms Organizations and Inspires Innovation* by Tim Brown

• *Creativity: Flow and the Psychology of Discovery and Invention* by Mihaly Csikszentmihalyi

• *Designing for Growth: A Design Thinking Toolkit for Managers* by Jeanne Liedtka and Tim Ogilvie

• *Disciplined Dreaming: A Proven System to Drive Breakthrough Creativity* by Josh Linkner

• *Gamestorming: A Playbook for Innovators, Rulebreakers, and Changemakers* by Dave Gray, Sunni Brown and James Macanufo

• *Implementing Change: Patterns, Principles, and Potholes* by Gene E. Hall and Shirley M. Hord

• *The Innovator's DNA: Mastering the Five Skills of Disruptive Innovators* by Jeff Dyer, Hal Gregersen and Clayton M. Christensen

• *Make Space: How to Set the Stage for Creative Collaboration* by Hasso Plattner Institute of Design at Stanford University and David Kelley

• *Managing Innovation: Integrating Technological, Market and Organizational Change* by Joe Tidd and John Bessant

• *Presentation Zen: Simple Ideas on Presentation Design and Delivery* by Garr Reynolds

• *slide:ology: The Art and Science of Creating Great Presentations* by Nancy Duarte

• *The Ten Faces of Innovation: IDEO's Strategies for Defeating the Devil's Advocate and Driving Creativity Throughout Your Organization* by Tom Kelley and Jonathan Littman

• *Unfolding the Napkin: The Hands-On Method for Solving Complex Problems with Simple Pictures* by Dan Roam

• *Visual Teams: Graphic Tools for Commitment, Innovation, and High Performance* by David Sibbet